THE
ENTREPRENEUR

The Way Back for the U.S. Economy

Robert Ringer

THRESHOLD EDITIONS

New York   London   Toronto   Sydney   New Delhi

Threshold Editions
A Division of Simon & Schuster, Inc.
1230 Avenue of the Americas
New York, NY 10020

First Threshold Editions hardcover edition July 2012

THRESHOLD EDITIONS and colophon are trademarks of Simon & Schuster, Inc.

For information about special discounts for bulk purchases, please contact Simon & Schuster Special Sales at 1-866-506-1949 or business@simonandschuster.com.

The Simon & Schuster Speakers Bureau can bring authors to your live event. For more information or to book an event, contact the Simon & Schuster Speakers Bureau at 1-866-248-3049 or visit our website at www.simonspeakers.com.

Manufactured in the United States of America

10   9   8   7   6   5   4   3   2   1

Library of Congress Cataloging-in-Publication Data

Ringer, Robert J.
  The entrepreneur : The way back for the U.S. economy / Robert Ringer.—
1st Threshold Editions hardcover ed.
    p.   cm.
  Includes bibliographical references.
  1. Entrepreneurship—United States.   2. Small business—United States—
Management.   3. United States—Economic policy.   I. Title.
  HB615.R547 2012
  338'.040973—dc23   2011053412

ISBN 978-1-4516-2911-8
ISBN 978-1-4516-2912-5 (ebook)

*Dedicated to the entrepreneurs of the world,
to whom Western civilization owes the
highest standard of living mankind has ever known*

Contents

THE
ENTREPRENEUR

INTRODUCTION

If you're going to take the time to read this book, I believe you have a right to know a little about my philosophical and ideological roots. I say this because it is these philosophical and ideological roots that form the foundation for the case I set forth on the following pages.

Most people know me as an author, interviewer, and speaker, but I also have entrepreneurial blood running through my veins. And that's an occupation that I'm especially proud of in a world overwhelmed by a tsunami of progressivism.

I am also what I would describe as a libertarian-centered conservative—heavily influenced by the works of Ayn Rand since my teens. I believe in the right of the individual to go as far as his talents and efforts can take him, and, just as important, the right of the exceptional individual to be allowed to be exceptional.

Thus, I guess you could say that my philosophical view of the world is the polar opposite of the progressive's. Let me make it clear that I do not see the Great Satan as Barack Obama, Nancy Pelosi, Harry Reid, or any other member of the gangster government that has helped to put a stranglehold on the producers of our country. The Great Satan is progressivism itself!

There is much disagreement on the precise definitions of, and differences between, the ideological terms *progressivism, socialism, Marxism, communism,* and *liberalism,* but the one thing the adherents of these ideologies all have in common is a belief in the use of force to make people conform to the moral standards of others in order to achieve the utopian society envisioned by those in power.

In other words, they believe that the government should be allowed to do whatever it damn well pleases, including maintaining absolute power over its citizens and redistributing wealth as it sees fit.

Historians generally credit Theodore Roosevelt, who founded the Progressive Party in 1912, with injecting progressivism into American politics in a major way. Astonishingly, in a 1910 presidential campaign speech, Roosevelt said:

We grudge no man a fortune in civil life if it is honorably obtained and well used. It is not even enough that it should have been gained without damage to the community. We should permit it to be gained only so long as the gaining represents gaining to the community. This, I know, implies a policy of a far more active governmental interference with social and economic conditions in this country than we have yet had, but I think we have got to face the fact that such an increase in governmental control is now necessary.[1]

Whenever politicians start using the word *we*, it's a clear signal that they are advocating governmental force to bring about change that those in power deem to be desirable. *That* is the essence of progressivism.

In reality, however, the term *progressivism* is a misnomer. Based on their words and actions, progressives are actually *retrogressives*, because their actions show that they hate progress. (From this point on, I will therefore use the more appropriate terms *Retrogressive, Retrogressives,* and *retrogressivism* instead of the misleading terms *progressive, progressives,* and *progressivism.*)

Rather than rejoicing in technological progress, the Retrogressive has fought what he ignorantly perceives to be man's "enslavement" by machines. This is ignorance at its worst. Will Durant had it right when he said, "It is not revolution but invention that will liberate the slave." The Retrogressive tends to be a clueless idealist who cannot seem to comprehend that it is the fruits of invention that have given man the capacity to move forward and improve his standard of living in exponential leaps and bounds.

Thus, the Retrogressive hated the invention of the light bulb. He hated the invention of the automobile. He hated the invention of the jetliner. Above all, the Retrogressive harbors enormous disdain for the Entrepreneur, who has an annoying habit of creating products that people want rather than those that the Retrogressive *believes* they should want. Make no mistake about it, the Retrogressive is the natural enemy of the Entrepreneur, and thus an enemy of human progress.

Durant defined human progress as "increasing control of the environment by life . . . the domination of chaos by mind and purpose, of matter by form or will." So, why would anyone want to stop human progress? In most cases, it's not a matter of evil intent. Rather, it's a combination of naiveté, ignorance, and arrogance. Unfortunately, this naiveté, ignorance, and arrogance have been moving the United States away from liberty and toward servitude for more than a hundred years.

And this, in turn, has stifled the Entrepreneur and prevented him from creating untold products and services that could enhance mankind's existence.

Core Principles

I believe that liberty is man's natural state, tyranny his natural enemy. The foundation of liberty is a concept commonly referred to as Natural Law. The underlying premise of Natural Law is that each individual owns his own life and therefore has the right to do whatever he chooses with that life, so long as he does not forcibly interfere with the lives of others. Everyone has an equal and absolute right to sovereignty over his own body and his own property, as well as the right to pursue his own happiness in any way he chooses.

No one—repeat, *no one*—has the authority to grant rights to anyone else, because human beings already possess all natural rights at birth. These rights include both personal and economic freedoms, and the only way such freedoms can be lost is if someone takes them away by force. The one right that an individual does not naturally possess is the right to violate someone else's liberty.

It logically follows, then, that people's lives and actions are their own responsibility, and not by even the broadest interpretation of the Constitution are they the responsibility of government or "society." Nowhere in the Constitution does it say it is the government's duty—or right—to fulfill the needs and desires of individual citizens. The primary moral justification for the existence of government is to protect its citizens from aggression, both domestic and foreign.

Though most people have strong beliefs about one or more "good causes," such beliefs represent nothing more than personal opinions and are therefore morally inferior to individual liberty. In a truly free society, liberty must be given a higher priority than all other objectives, including any and all so-called noble causes that certain people may deem to be worthy.

Freedom is not about government-enforced security and equality. On the contrary, freedom is about insecurity and inequality. To the extent people are free to pursue their own goals, their results will, of course, be unequal. The more government and society try to intervene in human affairs in an effort to equalize results, the less freedom people have.

The price of freedom is not only eternal vigilance, but also self-responsibility. And, make no mistake about it, self-responsibility means that no one has a right to anything other than what others are willing to pay him, without government interference, in exchange for his products or services.

Unfortunately, there are two realities that play havoc with the idealistic concept of freedom:

The first reality is that many individuals insist on having freedom on their terms, which often translates into a warped and childish notion of equality among all people. The aim of those who prate about "shared prosperity" and "the public welfare" is almost always the same: repression of individual freedom.

Nonetheless, many people believe they should be free to violate the liberty of others. In other words, when they espouse freedom, what they are really referring to is *their* freedom.

The second reality is the importance of certitudes in a civilized society. Civilization cannot exist without a generally accepted code of conduct, and it is the code of conduct of Western culture that has made it the most civilized and prosperous civilization in the history of mankind. (I use the term *generally accepted* because life—notwithstanding what many would like to believe—is not always black and white.)

Our desire for civility must be second only to our desire to be free. Unfortunately, since the hippie protests of the sixties, Western culture has deteriorated into a cesspool of anything-goes, take-this-job-and-shove-it antisocial dropouts. There is a stunning disrespect for anything that smacks of mainstream, and a seeming hatred for Western civilization itself.

Still, what young people crave are certitudes. They want to know that there are limits to acceptable behavior, both in the eyes of their parents and to society as a whole. They want to know that aggression will always be punished. They want to know that they will be rewarded not on the basis of ethnicity, but on the basis of merit.

Purist libertarians argue that a totally free society can exist only in an atmosphere of anarchy, but this notion conflicts with the reality that civilization cannot exist without a generally accepted code of conduct. When certitudes cease to exist, confusion reigns, and confusion and frustration are natural bedfellows. Together they lead to fear—fear of the unknowns that might fill the vacancies left by certitudes.

Ironically, the worst long-term effect of a society without certitudes is that in the wake of chaos, someone ultimately will come along and force order upon it. In other words, it's an environment that is ripe for dictatorship. When certitudes vanish, the disappearance of liberty cannot be far behind.

The Delicate Balance

To paraphrase Will Durant, social organization is the replacement of chaos with order. Unfortunately, social organization also brought us government, politicians, and a legal system that is very much out of whack. One of the great paradoxes of social organization is that in order to prevent someone with a distorted notion of freedom from trampling on the freedom of others, and to prevent antisocial behavior from undermining the certitudes of Western civilization, to one extent or another freedom must be restricted.[2]

At a minimum, pragmatism dictates that people must live within the generally agreed-upon framework of the civilization of which they are a part. In the case of Western civilization, that framework includes such virtues as self-responsibility, respect for the property of others, hard work, honesty, loyalty, proper hygiene and dress, temperance, civility, tolerance, persistence, thriftiness, planning for the future, self-discipline, a stable economic system, respect for elders, and reverence for the family unit.

But perhaps the most glaring trademark of Eurocentric culture is nonviolence, in contrast to most societies throughout the world. Western culture is, in fact, the most civilized way of life the world has ever known, and nonviolence is its centerpiece. While it is true that Western countries are not perfect—that they are hypocritical, harbor political systems that routinely violate both property and civil rights, and are sometimes guilty of committing aggression against other nations—they are head and shoulders above all other civilizations when it comes to nonviolence.

Thus, while liberty should always be our number-one priority, reality dictates that we should be ever vigilant about preserving our cherished Eurocentric way of life, even if it means sacrificing to a slight degree our purist libertarian beliefs.

To one extent or another, the freedom of those who are either intent on violating the freedom of others or determined to destroy the fabric of Western civilization must be curtailed. It's a delicate balancing act, to be sure, and one that needs to be closely and continuously monitored by rational adults who extol the virtues of freedom. The overriding rule is: When in doubt, always give the nod to liberty.

The Pendulum

The story of the human race is told in the ebb and flow of liberty and tyranny. Just as communists are wrong to believe they can change human nature and convince people to willingly give up their freedom and property, so, too, is it a mistake for defenders of liberty to believe they can convince all those who believe in the use of force to achieve some abstract "higher purpose" to believe in freedom.

Today, just as Friedrich A. Hayek warned more than a half century ago—and yours truly warned more than thirty years ago—we are traveling at mach speed down the road to serfdom. While the average American, grounded in Western values, has been going about his life—raising a family, trying to get ahead financially, and living the good life—Retrogressives have been relentlessly, and often covertly, implementing their road-to-serfdom agenda.

Finally, in 2008, they found their savior in a president

who combines the most destructive traits of Woodrow Wilson, Franklin D. Roosevelt, and Saul Alinsky. A master at the art of stealth Marxism, Barack Obama, once in office, moved swiftly to try to dismantle America's capitalist system. As a result, things are now looking very grim for the future of the United States. But, as you will see in the following pages, all is not lost.

Having said this, I should give you advance warning that this book is a Retrogressive's worst nightmare. The Retrogressive deplores the idea of people taking responsibility for their own lives and seeking success on their own merits. The Retrogressive's stock in trade is a nasty little collectivist creation that non-producers have come to know and love as *entitlement* (which I will be addressing in some detail).

To the Retrogressive, the Entrepreneur is the single biggest obstacle standing between him and his desire to remake the world in his own image. And because the Retrogressive is absolutely certain that his ideas are morally superior to those of the capitalist villains who produce goods and services in the marketplace, he has no qualms about using force to achieve his ends. As Andy Stern, president of the SEIU (Service Employees International Union), put it, "We like to say: We use the power of persuasion first. If it doesn't work, we try the persuasion of power." Make no mistake about it, the Retrogressive is serious about achieving his ends.

A word of caution before proceeding with Chapter 1:

Introduction

In the event you are a dyed-in-the-wool Retrogressive, I would strongly recommend that you return this book for a full refund and curl up by the fireplace with something a bit more soothing—*The Coming Insurrection* might do the trick.

Caveat emptor.

1.

THE ENTREPRENEUR AS HERO

Remember the infamous Iran-hostage "crisis" that ended after 444 days on January 20, 1981? With Jimmy Carter spending more than a year trying to figure out how to tie his shoelaces, the Evil Eye of Iran—Ayatollah Khomeini—had things pretty much his way.

But twenty minutes after Ronald Reagan was sworn in as president, Khomeini apparently started envisioning a nuclear cloud over Iran for the next four hundred years and decided to release the hostages. Like every other American, I was happy for both the hostages and their families.

Nevertheless, when the media started portraying them as heroes and New York held a ticker tape parade for them, I was puzzled. You happen to be in the wrong place at the wrong time, and you're hailed as a hero? Really?

Heroes are people who accomplish extraordinary feats under extraordinarily difficult circumstances, such as the firefighters who marched *into* the World Trade Center towers, in an attempt to save lives, while everyone else was scurrying to get out.

But there's another kind of hero—one who makes a living accomplishing extraordinary feats under extraordinarily difficult circumstances, day in and day out. The hero I'm referring to is an individualist known to all as the *Entrepreneur*.

The central focus of this book is twofold: (1) to explain

what it takes for an Entrepreneur to succeed and (2) to demonstrate how government meddling in the economy gets in the way of his creating products and services that people want—at the lowest possible prices.

Why the Entrepreneur to the exclusion of all others, such as employees, who also contribute to the growth of the economy? Because the Entrepreneur is perhaps the most misunderstood and underappreciated human being on earth.

Entrepreneurs come in all sizes, shapes, colors, genders, and ethnicities. Steve Wynn (gambling resort hotels), Howard Schultz (Starbucks), and, of course, Donald Trump are billionaires, but their lofty level of success doesn't strip them of their hero status as Entrepreneurs. When it comes to entrepreneurship, Wynn, Schultz, and Trump just happen to be size extra-large. Thus, while virtually all small businesspeople are Entrepreneurs, not all Entrepreneurs are small businesspeople.

However, when I use the term *Entrepreneur* in this book, unless otherwise stated I am referring primarily to the small-to-medium-sized Entrepreneur whose day-to-day eating habits are directly tied to what he produces. Unlike the salaried worker, the Entrepreneur has no safety net. He gets results or he starves.

It is not surprising that so many of our heroic Founding Fathers were Entrepreneurs. Perhaps the two most famous examples are George Washington and Thomas Jefferson. They are also good examples of just how far apart the results of individual Entrepreneurs can be. Though they were both farmers, Washington was one of the richest men in America, while Jefferson struggled financially throughout his life and died broke. But Jefferson's financial difficulties never dampened his enthusiasm for entrepreneurial pursuits, which resulted not only in the building of his beloved Monticello estate, but also in the establishment of one of America's most prestigious institutions of higher learning, the University of Virginia.

Being an Entrepreneur isn't for everyone. It takes a special combination of character traits: self-confidence, courage, boldness, self-reliance, resourcefulness, and persistence, to name a few of the more important ones. The Entrepreneur thrives on challenges and risk-taking. He is willing to venture outside the conventional-wisdom box, and his success is critical to his nation's prosperity.

Before I go further, let me make it clear that nothing in this book is meant to detract from the economic contributions of hundreds of millions of employees throughout the world who put in an honest day's work for an honest day's pay. Choosing to be an employee rather than an Entrepreneur is just another route to getting what you want in life.

As a general rule, an employee has less upside potential and more security than the Entrepreneur, while the Entrepreneur, at least in theory, has unlimited upside potential but little, if any, security. Where people get into trouble is when they want it all—the biggest upside potential coupled with rock-solid security. The nature of the marketplace—at least on planet Earth—makes these two objectives totally incompatible.

I would also like to point out that employees are *not* "associates." When the Walmarts of the world call their employees "associates," it is just another of the thousands of politically correct, Retrogressive ploys used to move us toward a utopian society where everyone is equal.

Personally, I find this practice insulting to the intelligence of employees. During my short stints as an employee in my younger years, I *knew* I was an employee, and I was quite happy to be one. I wasn't interested in being humored with a politically correct title. My focus was on doing the best job I could do in the hopes of getting a pay raise. Please, Retrogressives, spare us the "associate" stuff.

But here's the nice thing about living in a free country. (Hopefully, you're old enough to remember living in a free country.) A person can start out as an employee—and most people do—then, when he believes he's ready, he can choose to leave his job and go into business for himself. The advantage in doing this is that when he leaves, he takes with him all the knowledge and skills he accumulated while being paid to do his job.

Striking out on one's own is a risk-reward choice, and, in a free society, it's a choice that's open to everyone. Under capitalism, it's possible for anyone to start as a low-level employee and rise to the top through his own efforts. Some people start out as employees, strike out on their own, fail, and return to the job market—either temporarily or for life. Others, like Wynn and Schultz, go on to great entrepreneurial success—even becoming billionaires.

The Ticket Scalper

One of my favorite Entrepreneurs is the ticket scalper. He doesn't need an office, employees, a formal education, or specialized skills. His main assets are his willingness to hustle and take risks. He epitomizes what the free market is all about. He is living proof that a black market is nothing more than the free market asserting itself in the face of government oppression.

The ticket scalper acquires his inventory at the lowest possible prices, then sells at the highest prices the market will bear. If a ticket scalper works hard at his craft and is blessed with a bit of good luck, he can make a substantial amount of money. But when myriad factors go against him (weather, for example), he can end up going home with a handful of worthless tickets. Thus, the ticket scalper's success is far from guaranteed. His is the risk-taking life of the Entrepreneur.

One other point worth mentioning about ticket scalpers: A majority of them are African-Americans. That's scary, right? I mean, what would you do if one of those tough-looking dudes refused to give you the correct change or even sold you counterfeit tickets? No wonder ticket scalping is technically illegal outside virtually all stadiums and arenas.

To the Retrogressive who believes that government regulation is necessary to protect consumers from ticket scalpers—primarily black ticket scalpers—I have bad news for you. In the scores of times I have dealt with ticket scalpers over the years, I have never been cheated out of a dime. Not even once.

In fact, in every case I can think of—no matter how heated the haggling became—once our transaction was completed, the ticket scalper has never failed to cheerfully say something to me like "Enjoy the game."

A ticket scalper knows that if he isn't totally honest in his dealings with the public, he will soon become an outcast among his peers. Like insurance companies and banks, ticket scalpers have to protect the reputation of their industry. Free-market self-regulation beats government regulation every time. No exceptions.

The Street Performer

I recently returned from speaking at an investment conference in New Orleans. On the Sunday that the conference ended, my wife and I walked around the French Quarter and watched some of the street acts. What struck me was that the people who put on those acts, much like ticket scalpers, are engaged in unfettered capitalism—and most of them are black.

On one street corner we came upon a somewhat rotund, middle-aged woman by the name of Doreen Ketchens, who was alternately playing the clarinet and singing. Her talent at each was as good as any I have ever seen. Her rendition of "Stormy Weather" sent chills up my spine.

Listeners who were so inclined put money in her basket

to show their appreciation. And as I watched cash flowing into the basket, it occurred to me that the perverted mind of the Retrogressive might see this as a degrading way to make a living. But I saw it as very dignified work, which was evidenced by Doreen's proud demeanor. Plain and simple, Doreen Ketchens engages in free-market transactions with consenting adults. No government bureaucrats need intervene, thank you.

And she is just one of the many remarkably talented acrobats, comedians, singers, and musicians—most of them black—who prefer entrepreneurship in the French Quarter to government handouts as a way to get what they want out of life.

Isn't it amazing how consenting adults are able to transact business with one another without government involvement? It boggles the imagination to think about how the marketplace would explode with economic activity and jobs if the government would just stop regulating, taxing, and giving people incentives not to work—in short, if the government would get the hell out of the way. I'm referring here to nothing less than a totally laissez-faire economy.

The truth is that the Retrogressive does not want blacks to be too well off. After all, what would he and his bureaucratic cronies do for a living if there were no more poverty? The black Entrepreneur is anathema to the far left.

The antithesis of the Entrepreneur is government employees, most of whom perform services that people do not want or that can be done better, and more efficiently, by the private sector.

Nevertheless, honesty compels me to be somewhat of an apologist for government employees. Most, I believe, are simply victims of the Retrogressive's big-government trap. Weaned on the notion that government is inherently good, and that government services are necessary in order to implement certain vague notions of "fairness," they truly believe they are engaged in the noblest of all professions: public service.

They do not realize that they are being used as pawns—voting pawns. As the Retrogressives in all three branches of government continue to mislead and obfuscate in an effort to decrease employment in the private sector and increase government employment, they get ever closer to their decades-long goal of securing a foolproof, permanent majority of voters—which translates into perpetual power.

The True Entrepreneur

When I use the term *Entrepreneur,* I am referring to a *true* entrepreneur—an entrepreneur who does his best to avoid government favors and financial largesse to advance his agenda. I say *does his best,* because the cards are stacked in such a way as to force everyone to rely on government to one extent or another.

A perfect example of this is roads and highways. Since virtually all roads and highways are government owned, even the most staunch libertarian has no choice but to use them. A Retrogressive would therefore take great delight in calling such a person a hypocrite. This is an old trick used by the "gotcha" Retrogressive: Have the government take control of the postal service, healthcare, etc.—then wave aside the libertarian-centered conservative as a hypocrite for using these government-provided services.

Yes, all Entrepreneurs use government-provided services at one time or another, but that doesn't change the fact that, left alone to do what they do best, they grow the economy, provide jobs, and—through the "invisible hand of the marketplace"—improve the lives of millions of people whom they will never even meet. In fact, when it comes to jobs, anyone who watches the news knows that small-business owners create 75 percent of all new jobs in America. Take a look at these eye-opening statistics:

By themselves, the goods, services and technology produced by American small businesses make up the world's third-largest economy, after the United States and Japan. Small companies represent 99 percent of all U.S. businesses and employ more than half of the American workforce. According to the U.S. Small Business Administration: Small businesses pay more than 44 percent of the nation's private payroll. More than 50 percent of the U.S. private gross domestic product is generated by small business, and almost 97 percent of exporters are small businesses.[1]

America's Entrepreneurs have managed to do all this on their own, relying as little as possible on the government.

Another thing that distinguishes the true Entrepreneur from the average individual who trades hours for dollars is that he tends to be impatient—especially when it comes to being slowed down.

I've come to grudgingly accept the fact that most people are urgency challenged. Which is why, in today's world, the individual who displays a sense of urgency stands out like a thinking person at a Barack Obama rally. A lot of people take umbrage at this sense of urgency, because it gets in the way of their enjoying their favorite reality TV shows and weekend sports telethons. Folks who want things done sooner rather than later irritate them no end.

Why is sooner rather than later so important? Because every one of us has to deal with an irreplaceable, finite commodity known as *time*. The entrepreneurial mind gets this; the nonentrepreneurial mind does not. The Entrepreneur's mind-set is: "Just get out of my way and I'll do it myself!" The Entrepreneur doesn't want to know what someone else is *going* to do. He wants to know what he's *done*. He knows that spending hours each night kicking back and enjoying life may be a great way to reduce stress, but it does nothing to create wealth or jobs.

I can't tell you how many deals I've closed, how many projects made it through the open window, because I took action one month sooner, one week sooner, or one day sooner. Even an hour—sometimes even a minute—can be the difference between success and failure. This makes urgency one of the many traits that make the Entrepreneur so invaluable to the wealth of a nation, a trait that sets him apart from the nine-to-fiver.

In the Preface to Stephen M. R. Covey's book *The Speed of Trust,* his father, Stephen R. Covey (of *Seven Habits* fame), makes this remarkable statement: "My interactions with business leaders around the world have made it increasingly evident that 'speed to market' is now the ultimate competitive weapon."

Just think about that for a moment—the *ultimate* competitive weapon is speed. *The* most important thing an Entrepreneur can do to win out over the competition is get his product to market *fast.*

The Entrepreneur instinctively knows—or learns quickly through experience—that it's not how much money he makes, but how much money he makes in a given period of time. Say that two people each make a million dollars. One makes his million dollars in a year's time, while the other makes his million over the course of a forty-year career.

The latter person would have had an average annual income of $25,000—well below the poverty line. But the one who made his million dollars in a year is in the top 1 percent of income earners.

The Entrepreneur's sense of urgency is the antithesis of the union worker's mind-set. The Entrepreneur tries to deliver more value in less time. But a union worker who tries to work faster than his comrades is soon called on the carpet by his supervisor. Working too fast makes everyone else look bad, so labor unions insist that their members pay close attention to official signals for coffee breaks, lunch breaks, and quitting time. Sure worked out well for GM and Chrysler, didn't it? If the Entrepreneur thought this way, we would still be living in the Stone Age.

Andy Stern, president of the SEIU, one of Barack Obama's favorite Marxist organizations, and a frequent visitor to the White House, likes to mug Karl Marx by saying, "Workers of the world, unite" is "not just a slogan anymore." But Entrepreneurs have no interest in uniting. They're too busy creating wealth—wealth that the SEIUs of the world expropriate to feed their flocks of nonproducers.

The Issue of Trust

Am I suggesting that we should consider all Entrepreneurs heroes? Of course not. There are crooked Entrepreneurs out there, just as there are crooked employees, crooked clergymen, crooked athletes, and—alert the media!—crooked politicians.

Tony Rezko was an Entrepreneur who apparently made a lot of money through political connections (as a prominent fundraiser for then-senator Barack Obama and Illinois governor Rod Blagojevich) before being convicted and sent to prison for fraud and money laundering. A dishonest Entrepreneur . . . and definitely not a hero.

Bernie Madoff, too, was an Entrepreneur in that he organized and managed an enterprise with considerable initiative and took great risks—one of them being the risk of going to prison for life! But he was a *dishonest* Entrepreneur who defrauded people out of billions of dollars. Definitely not a hero.

I believe that the honest Entrepreneur has an inherent belief in liberty, while the dishonest Entrepreneur often believes in tyranny (e.g., using government force to gain an advantage over his competitors in the marketplace). It is the dishonest Entrepreneur who is the black sheep of an otherwise proud culture of heroes. Those who use government to gain an advantage in the marketplace bring dishonor to the good name of the Entrepreneur.

But let's be careful here. I've seen more than one falling out between two parties to a business deal where each believed that the other person acted dishonestly. One man's entrepreneurial saint is another man's entrepreneurial sinner. The difference can be, and usually is, in the eyes of the beholder—or is decided in a court of law.

So just because one or more people believe that an individual is dishonest doesn't mean he is. I feel obliged to make this point because too many far-left types seem to believe that anyone who becomes wealthy through the capitalist system does so only by "exploiting" others. The notion of a hardworking Entrepreneur becoming wealthy by providing great products and services at prices his customers are willing to pay undermines their belief in the supremacy of the state. That being said, throughout this book you can assume that whenever I use the term *Entrepreneur,* I am referring to the *honest* Entrepreneur.

In *The Speed of Trust,* Stephen M. R. Covey takes the speed issue a giant step beyond his father's statement that "speed to market" is now the ultimate competitive weapon. He says that the greatest catalyst for speed is *trust.* Where there is a lack of trust, says Covey, everything takes longer and costs more. And he's absolutely right. In today's fast-moving world, it's speed, not size, that carries the day—and, as the tired cliché goes, "levels the playing field," giving David the best chance he's had against Goliath since he used that homemade slingshot. After all, isn't it a lot faster and less expensive if you trust someone enough to make a deal on a handshake rather than having to bring in a brigade of problem-finding, fee-building attorneys to cross the t's and dot the i's?

Covey emphasizes that it's not so much how people act in the presence of others, it's what they do behind the scenes. (Anyone who doesn't understand why this is so probably shouldn't be reading this book.) And the successful Entrepreneur instinctively realizes that it's in his best interest to strive for consistency between what he says and does behind closed doors and how he presents himself in public. As I mentioned with regard to ticket scalpers, the Entrepreneur cannot afford the cost of not being trustworthy. So, sorry Retrogressives, but most Entrepreneurs are honest.

Entrepreneurial Traits

As I said earlier, Entrepreneurs come in all sizes, shapes, colors, genders, and ethnicities. Some Entrepreneurs believe in God; some are atheists. Some are kind and compassionate; some are ruthless. Some display great civility; some are uncouth. Some are faithful to their spouses; some are philanderers.

Each Entrepreneur is a unique human being with his own moral standards and his particular set of human frailties. As with Christians, Jews, Hindus, men, women, blacks, Hispanics, and people of all ethnicities, certain generalizations are valid. But each *individual* is unique.

With that caveat, I would like to point out some generalizations—repeat, *generalizations*—that I believe to be valid for most Entrepreneurs. To name but a few of the obvious ones, Entrepreneurs generally believe in hard work, long hours, short-term sacrifice to achieve long-term gain, the power to control one's own destiny, and individual sovereignty.

Thus, the true Entrepreneur is everything the collectivist is not—self-sufficient, a risk-taker, and an individualist. Unfortunately, these traits make him the target of jealousy, vilification, intimidation, bullying, and even blackmail.

The Entrepreneur is driven by the desire to create wealth for himself. So how does that make him a hero?

For one thing, successful Entrepreneurs stay in business. As a result of their pursuit of profits, they create more jobs, produce more products and services that people want, and do the one thing that government can *never* do: stimulate the economy. It is just one of the many reasons capitalism results in a better life for the greatest number of people, which I will discuss in great detail in Chapter 4.

Is there anyone in this day and age—even the most ardent Retrogressive—who does not understand this self-evident truth? Scary to contemplate, but, yes, I believe there are millions of folks who do not understand it—most of them well-meaning but ignorant. Even so, they are no less dangerous to the well-being of a nation than those who are informed but malevolent.

Further, the successful Entrepreneur pays more taxes than the average worker, but don't tell that to those who want to control everyone's life through a corrupted web of government largesse. And, as Arthur Laffer demonstrated decades ago with his famous Laffer Curve, lower taxes stimulate economic activity, which in turn increases both the profits *and* taxes paid by the Entrepreneur.

All well and good, but doesn't the Entrepreneur always act in his own self-interest? Absolutely! And so does everyone else in this neck of our galaxy. Do you believe that politicians do not act in their own self-interest—that they do not pass laws and regulations intended to keep themselves in office and live luxuriously at the taxpayers' expense?

Likewise, spreading what they believe to be the spiritual truth makes clergymen happy. When they do so, they act in their rational self-interest and, like the Entrepreneur, make others happy in the process.

Adam Smith's "invisible hand" doesn't just bring about wonders in the marketplace. It works in all areas of life. If the Retrogressive would just stop trying to play God by carrying on a nonstop fight against universal law, life would be so much easier for everyone.

The fact is that self-interest is neither good nor bad. It's simply a human trait. The Entrepreneur acts in his own self-interest by producing goods and services that other people want, which he hopes will increase his own wealth and well-being.

Those who are parasitic—who live off the efforts of others—also act in their own self-interest. The former is an example of *rational* self-interest, while the latter is an example of *irrational* self-interest. The Entrepreneur's self-interest is a benefit to society as a whole, while the self-interest of those who are parasitic is a drag on the economy and the productive efforts of others.

For this reason alone, even if you're not an Entrepreneur, you should cheer for the success of those who are. The Entrepreneur is not your enemy; he is your friend. Not because he wants to control your life, but because he understands that the best way to get what he wants is to give you what *you* want.

The Entrepreneur knows that if he does not give you the best products and services at the lowest possible prices, his competitors will be more than happy to win your patronage by doing so. How do you think big, bad Walmart got to where it is today—by selling inferior products and services at the *highest* possible prices? Sam Walton is a great example of an ambitious, hardworking Entrepreneur who ended up building a goliath company by giving people what they wanted.

By creating jobs and stimulating the economy, the Entrepreneur helps the underprivileged more than any politician or government program could ever hope to do. This alone makes him a hero in every sense of the word. It also makes him the enemy of the Retrogressive, because it undermines the Retrogressive's agenda for achieving power over others through government wealth-transfer programs.

Though it's difficult for well-meaning do-gooders to understand, most politicians are not interested in helping the underprivileged. Rather, they see them as faceless, expendable, less-than-human creatures who not only can be bribed into voting for them, but can be used for photo ops when needed. (Jimmy Carter and John Edwards come quickly to mind.)

Perhaps John F. Kennedy's most memorable statement was "And so, my fellow Americans, ask not what your country can do for you, ask what you can do for your country." Sounds patriotic, to be sure. But many an innocent person has been led down the road to serfdom by such high-sounding sloganeering. Kennedy's statement is one that deserves a full-fledged debate by those on both sides of the issue, so, to avoid getting sidetracked, we'll leave that for another day.

The reason I bring it up here is that it gives me a platform to present my view of how the Entrepreneur best serves his country. In my opinion, the most valuable contribution anyone can make to his fellow man is to produce products and services that others want and, as a result, not only be a self-sustaining individual but, in the process, create jobs and stimulate the economy. I emphasize the words *as a result.*

This is what the Entrepreneur excels at, and why he can feel proud in the knowledge that he is among those individuals on our planet who are not adding to its problems. It is, above all else, what makes him a bona fide hero.

Unfortunately, the government harbors great disdain for the Entrepreneur, especially the small Entrepreneur. Why? Because he is stubbornly independent. He doesn't need or want government help. The Entrepreneur makes his own way in the world.

In a truly free society, it would be difficult enough for the Entrepreneur to make a profit. Much like an orchestra conductor, he has to be on top of every aspect of his enterprise. He has to make sure that every employee is doing his job correctly.

And when he goes broke—as millions of small businesspeople have done—he often feels like all he has to show for his work is that he provided a lot of good jobs for his employees for an extended period of time. They go on to the next job, while he goes on to face his creditors.

Ironically, the Entrepreneur's biggest threat is also his biggest employee—the government. I say *biggest employee* because the government is supposed to work for *him.* It says so in that antiquated little piece of work called the

Constitution. But those who hold the reins of power don't much care about the Constitution.

As a result, the government taxes the Entrepreneur at every turn, regulates him to death (often literally), and relentlessly harasses him. Rather than being his humble servant, the government has transformed itself into the natural predator of the Entrepreneur.

Some people marvel at how far mankind has advanced in such a short period of time. But what they marvel at is not a reflection of his true potential; it is his true potential *minus* government interference. It is hard to fathom where mankind might be today had government never been allowed to go beyond its original purpose of protecting the lives and property of its citizens.

2.

PUTTING IT ALL ON THE LINE

The ever-quotable seventeenth-century Jesuit priest Baltasar Gracian said it eloquently: "Have stomach for the large morsels of fortune. . . . Great accomplishments are built on great capacity. . . . There are many who cannot enjoy highly seasoned dishes because of their natural limitations, neither having been born to, or having been accustomed to, such high fare." [1]

Most people simply do not have the capacity to think big thoughts, let alone convert those thoughts into action. The ultimate nightmare for such people is waking up some fine morning only to discover that they're going in the opposite direction from that in which the mainstream is headed.

To people with a lemming mentality, acceptance is more important than money, dignity, or purpose. Which is unfortunate, because success and the desire for acceptance are mutually exclusive objectives. The Entrepreneur gets used to not being accepted—not to mention being derided and vilified.

Risk-taking and Failure

It's difficult for the Retrogressive to comprehend the mind-set of the Entrepreneur. I'm talking about the willingness to risk everything in exchange for being one's own boss and having the opportunity—*not* the guarantee—to make a lot more money than would be possible in a nine-to-five job. It's a big part of the price the Entrepreneur pays for having that big upside potential. And it's one of the many traits that separate him from the wage earner or the individual who exchanges hours for dollars (such as accountants and attorneys).

Unless a person is willing to put it all on the line, he should not even consider venturing into the world of the Entrepreneur. Because if the Entrepreneur fails, he can lose everything. By *everything,* I'm not just referring to his savings, his stocks, his collectibles, and his kids' college funds. I'm talking about his house, his furniture, his cars—everything he owns. Not to mention his credit, his self-esteem, and, all too often, his "friends." The Retrogressive who spews out down-with-capitalism rhetoric has no idea of the full extent of the risks the Entrepreneur takes in an effort to achieve success.

Many of the most successful people in our nation's history have lost everything, or come close to it, by putting everything they owned on the line because they believed so strongly in what they were doing. Walt Disney, for example, nearly went bankrupt while working on several of his early movies, including *Snow White and the Seven Dwarfs, Pinocchio,* and *Fantasia.*

I should mention that, to a certain extent, those who sell their services by the hour are entrepreneurial in that they have to build a client list, then satisfy those clients in order to secure repeat business—plus, in some cases, they have substantial overhead. But it's not quite the same as someone who goes into a venture that is based on an idea and puts everything on the line by betting he can convert that idea into a profitable venture.

And that's what sets him apart. If there were no risks involved, everyone would be an Entrepreneur. The Entrepreneur fully understands that if he fails, he will get hurt—often badly. But he is not afraid of failure. In fact, he realizes that failure is actually a good thing because it serves as a positive learning experience.

I once read a fascinating article in the *Wall Street Journal* that explained that most hi-tech venture capitalists preferred to back Silicon Valley Entrepreneurs who had gone broke once or twice rather than those who had not yet ventured out on their own. Their thinking was that the individual who has already tried and failed has some seasoning. He already knows many of the pitfalls, which puts him in a position to make better decisions.

Those who look down on Entrepreneurs who have failed have no understanding of how treacherous the road to success can be. As previously mentioned, Thomas Jefferson died broke—and was broke most of his life—but you'd have a tough time trying to convince anyone that he was a failure.

Glenn Beck is a great modern-day example of an Entrepreneur who has managed to overcome a string of self-inflicted failures to achieve remarkable success. After hitting rock bottom in 2001, Beck rose to unprecedented heights in the world of television and now heads up Mercury Radio Arts, a live streaming video network that employs more than a hundred people.

Then there's multimillionaire Chris Gardner. Just about everyone knows his story, which includes sleeping on the floor in a subway restroom with his son, because there was a movie made about it—*The Pursuit of Happyness*. Gardner says that he learned from his grandmother, at a very young age, that "the cavalry ain't comin'." As he says, everyone has one thing he can always fall back on: his butt. And that's exactly where most Entrepreneurs have landed— usually many times.

Robert Kiyosaki, the phenomenally successful author of *Rich Dad, Poor Dad,* was once so broke that he and his wife had to sleep in their car. It is beyond the comprehension of the Retrogressive that a human being could come back from homelessness and succeed—*without* government help.

But the Entrepreneur has the mental toughness to pick himself up, brush himself off, and move on to the next deal. And when he moves on, he does so with an arsenal of newly acquired knowledge and wisdom.

The Entrepreneur may go through this painful ordeal many times, but when he finally succeeds, society as a whole benefits from his efforts. That's a pretty good deal for those who remain on the sidelines, which is yet another big reason the Entrepreneur should be looked upon as a hero.

What the Retrogressive does not understand is that people must be *allowed* to fail. As the remarkable Holocaust survivor Viktor Frankl, who lost his entire family in Nazi concentration camps, put it, man has a *right* to fail. Not only is it not the government's moral prerogative to protect anyone from failure, it has no constitutional right to do so.

In his ignorant, arrogant, and naïve view of the world, the Retrogressive wants life to be risk free for everyone. But when you take away the right to fail, you take away creativity and resourcefulness. If the Retrogressive had his way, nothing would ever be created.

Robert Kiyosaki put it well when he said, "Winners are not afraid of losing. But losers are. Failure is part of the process of success. People who avoid failure also avoid success." I would go even further and say that success is not possible without failure. Remember the ad in which Michael Jordan admitted that he'd missed something like twenty-two game-winning shots, then concluded by saying, "I succeed because I fail"?

The Entrepreneur embraces failure, because he understands that each failure brings him one step closer to success. And it goes without saying that the honest Entrepreneur does not want government help when he fails. On the contrary, what he wants is for the government to leave him alone.

Things Change

The great libertarian economist Henry Hazlitt once said that the success of an Entrepreneur is highly dependent on his ability to predict the future. What an interesting—and, to many, scary—thought. Predicting the future is serious business—Nostradamus stuff. And the only thing the Entrepreneur knows about the future with absolute certainty is that circumstances always change. Do you remember when it seemed as though . . .

- No one could possibly rival Sears—until Walmart came along?

- No one could possibly rival Waldenbooks—until Barnes & Noble came along?

- Nothing could possibly rival the Palm Pilot—until the BlackBerry came along?

- Nothing could possibly rival the Walkman—until the iPod came along?

And how about the invention of the modern air conditioner? In the 1940s it was the catalyst for a population explosion in the unbearably hot South and Southwest. Cities like Dallas, Houston, Atlanta, and Miami became major metropolises and changed the face of America forever. Entrepreneurs who saw it coming made fortunes.

Then, of course, there are the two catastrophic events that changed *everything*—9/11 and, less than eight years later, the arrival of Barack Obama and his army of Retrogressive allies in Washington. Ayn Rand's warnings, once fodder for liberal snickering, have become today's reality.

Things change—which makes predicting the future a tough proposition. To make matters worse, the past is not a sure indicator of the future, as evidenced by the stock and real estate markets. Contrary to what "chartists" would have us believe, the past movement of a stock or a market is not a reliable indicator of whether it will go up or down in the future. By acting on the assumption that it is, you base your investment decisions on a false premise.

This is precisely what occurred with the infamous dotcom collapse of the late nineties and early 2000s, as well as the overall market collapse of 2008.

An example of a false assumption that probably led many Entrepreneurs astray decades ago was that computers would dramatically reduce the amount of paper we use. Virtually everyone held this view in the early years of the computer age, but it turned out to be dead wrong. Instead, computers have had the exact opposite effect and have drowned us in a sea of paper beyond anything we could have imagined.

One of the Entrepreneur's greatest challenges, then, is to make accurate assumptions when it comes to predicting the future, then have the self-confidence and courage to put everything on the line to back up his belief that his assumptions are correct.

Betting the Farm

The Entrepreneur does not fear change, even though it often wreaks havoc with his plans. He recognizes that change can bring with it great opportunities. He is willing to shove all his chips to the center of the table and place a bet on the outcome, which often means betting the farm, literally. It's a hazardous undertaking in which good intentions don't count for much. Nature punishes us just as harshly when we are stupid but well-intentioned as when we are smart but malevolent. Either way, universal law delivers to us the results we deserve.

Of course, to the Retrogressive, this is incomprehensible. Why would anyone want to spend an enormous amount of his time, energy, and money, knowing that he might end up with nothing? Why would he be willing to assume all the risk, without the slightest safety net provided by the government?

Answer: to make a lot of money! That's what motivates Entrepreneurs. Not helping people . . . not "saving the world" . . . not protecting the human race from global cooling or global warming (whichever happens to be in vogue at any given time).

None of this means that the Entrepreneur does not care about these things. It does not mean he is not civic minded. It does not mean he is not charitable. It's just that none of these have anything to do with his chief *business* objective—making money.

As it happens, there is a connection between an Entrepreneur's financial success and the likelihood that he will contribute to charity. But it has nothing to do with business. The connection is that financial success is what makes charitable contributions possible. And common sense, in addition to history, tells us that the more successful a person's business is, the more charitable he is likely to be.

Think of Bill Gates giving $29 billion to start a foundation to help fight disease and poverty in Africa. Or Andrew Carnegie, a century ago, building libraries nationwide that now benefit all of society. For most of this country's history, it has been super-successful Entrepreneurs like Henry Ford, John D. Rockefeller, and Andrew Mellon who have set up our great charitable foundations. They didn't need a government club over their heads to get them to share their wealth. They did it voluntarily, out of a personal desire to help their fellow man.

But what if they had not shared their wealth voluntarily? The answer to that hypothetical question is one that the Retrogressive cannot accept: It's *their* wealth, so what they do with it is no one else's business. What someone else *thinks* they should do with it is but a personal opinion.

Some might argue that great philanthropists have given to charity just to assuage their own egos. Perhaps. But what does it matter if the charitable result is the same?

And keep in mind that charity is not the only social

benefit that results from successful entrepreneurship. Again, the sole purpose of a business enterprise is to make as much money as possible, and the more money a business makes, the more capital it has to expand and the more people it can afford to hire.

When a business is profitable, unemployment decreases and the economy expands. Pretty nice that it all works out so well, isn't it? No government intervention necessary, thank you.

The Action Factor

When it comes to putting it all on the line, what it really boils down to is the willingness to take action. If there is one thing above all others that separates the Entrepreneur from the non-entrepreneurs of the world, it is his high ratio of action to words.

The Entrepreneur doesn't wait until "the time is right" to strike out on his own. He understands that the time is *never* "right." He knows that the best time to take action is *now*. Not next month, not next week, not tomorrow—NOW!

That he will make mistakes is a certainty. But action puts him in a position to learn from, and correct, his mistakes as he goes along.

Great Entrepreneurs don't allow themselves to get caught up in the "what-if" trap—attempting to project every problem and every solution in advance of taking action. They can make fairly accurate assumptions about what is likely to happen, but they know that things change.

That's why they don't spend an inordinate amount of time and effort trying to develop the perfect business plan. As General Patton put it, "A good plan today is better than a perfect plan tomorrow." To the action-oriented Entrepreneur, a rough outline on the back of a napkin will do just fine. (In fact, neither Google nor Microsoft had any business plan at all when they started.)

This is very different from the approach of most wannabe Entrepreneurs. Instead of taking action, they have a remarkable ability to come up with ingenious excuses for procrastinating. An acquaintance of mine, well into his sixties, once told me that even though he became financially secure by working for big corporations all his life, he regretted not having left the corporate world and gone out on his own. He lamented that no matter how much money he made, he always felt like he was "a highly paid slave."

That wasn't the first time I had heard such a lamentation. But guess what? Every person who claims to regret not having gone out on his own had a choice. Golden handcuffs in the corporate world are not locked. The individual has it within his power to slip out of them at any time if he has entrepreneurial blood flowing through his veins.

In this regard, the late and legendary Joe Karbo was able to sell millions of copies of his self-published book *The Lazy Man's Way to Riches* through a brilliantly

conceived advertising campaign. The blockbuster head-
line to his full-page newspaper ads reads: MOST PEOPLE
ARE TOO BUSY EARNING A LIVING TO MAKE ANY
MONEY.

When I first read Karbo's headline, I envisioned millions of people coast to coast shaking their heads up and
down. That's because a paycheck is the only thing standing
between most people and their ultimate nightmare: If they
can't make the payments on their shiny new SUV and big-
screen HD television set, the Snootsuns across the street
might just discover the bloody truth about them. Bless that
bill-paying, nine-to-five job.

So, what does Mr. Burbs do when he gets home from
work? Does he sit down in front of his not-yet-paid-for
big-screen TV, have a glass of wine, relax, enjoy a quiet
candlelight dinner, then work on serious-moneymaking
endeavors the rest of the evening?

Not likely. When he sets foot inside his home, the only
thing on his mind is dealing with the daily clutter of life—
from the trouble Johnny got into at school that day to un-
paid bills to the packet of information on his mutual fund
that came in the mail.

Mr. Burbs's biggest challenge is to deal with this tidal
wave of clutter as quickly as possible so he can get to bed
at a reasonable hour. After all, servitude is not an easy job.
One has to be rested in order to perform tomorrow's duties.

Now and then, he fantasizes about working on money-
making entrepreneurial projects on the weekend. Which is

a nice thought, but it rarely happens, because the weekend is his only chance to catch up on the clutter that he wasn't able to get to during the week:

Mowing the lawn . . . changing the air filters in his house . . . gassing and washing the cars . . . dropping off and picking up the dry cleaning . . . reinstalling Windows on his dying computer . . . helping Johnny with a massive, but totally meaningless, project that is due in Ms. Malevolent's class on Monday . . . and so it goes.

The result, of course, is that Mr. Burbs, notwithstanding his good intentions, never quite gets around to working on the entrepreneurial plan of his dreams. The story of Mr. Burbs is that he ultimately gives up all hope of becoming an Entrepreneur and instead focuses on trying to get a pay raise.

Unlike wannabe Entrepreneurs like Mr. Burbs, the true Entrepreneur comes to the realization, sooner rather than later, that his escape from "prison" begins with understanding that he himself possesses the mental key to unlock his prison door. Once he acknowledges that reality, he is prepared to risk everything in exchange for the unlimited upside potential. He has no intention of spending the rest of his life reflecting on the words of John Greenleaf Whittier: "The saddest words of tongue or pen are these: 'It might have been.'"

The Entrepreneur knows that he cannot afford to procrastinate, and that without action, neither freedom nor success is possible. Further, he knows that most of the things people worry about never come to pass—and even when they do, they usually end up not being nearly as bad as envisioned. Even better, they often turn out to be nothing more than great opportunities in disguise.

The Retrogressive is incapable of understanding the motivation that drives the Entrepreneur, the enormous risks he takes, or how his efforts benefit the overall economy. It is this ignorance that causes him to see the Entrepreneur as a villain, as someone whose success comes at the expense of others.

The truth, of course, is quite the opposite, but we'll get into that later in detail. For now, suffice it to say that the Entrepreneur is a hero for being willing to put everything on the line in pursuit of a better life, because the better his life, the more he benefits society as a whole. In a sane world inhabited by rational, nonenvious human beings, the Entrepreneur's willingness to take risks and act quickly would be applauded by all. But, alas, we do not live in a sane world. We live in a world where politicians and bureaucratic hacks see the Entrepreneur as a threat to their hold on power.

3.

WHATEVER IT TAKES

When he was a very young boy, I gave my son a Lucite cube that displayed the words WHATEVER IT TAKES! To this day, that cube sits atop his dresser as a constant reminder that in the world in which we actually live—not the make-believe world of the Retrogressive—success is directly tied to a person's willingness to do whatever it takes to succeed. When I look back over my career, almost every success I've had can be traced to my willingness to go far beyond what I knew others were willing to do.

The Retrogressive, on the other hand, believes that everyone should be rewarded just for being alive. The Entrepreneur instinctively recognizes that if the rules of the game made everyone's results equal, life would be devoid of meaning. And therein lies the basis for the perpetual ideological war between the Retrogressive and the Entrepreneur. The former relentlessly connives to eliminate the incentive for individuals to get ahead on their own merits and hard work, while the latter believes that one's own merits and hard work should be the key determinants in one's success.

To believe there can be a compromise between these two fundamentally different viewpoints is naïve to an extreme. The ideological war between the Entrepreneur and the Retrogressive has existed throughout recorded history, and is likely to continue until the last human breath on earth is extinguished. The only way results can be equalized is through the use of force, and force is never acceptable to men of goodwill.

While college kids and other young adults may be excused for youthful exuberance and a lack of knowledge and experience, it can be assumed that the adult Retrogressive, fully aware that equalization of results is possible only through the use of force, does not act out of goodwill toward his fellow man. Rather, his actions are based on an alarming arrogance wherein he has convinced himself that he is morally superior to others and therefore in a much better position to decide who must give, how much he should give, and who should be on the receiving end.

Entrepreneurship 101

When I was about twenty years old, I learned firsthand what "whatever it takes" really means. I wanted to earn as much money as possible before going back to school in the fall, so I decided to open a produce stand—a little shack painted fire-engine red, with a dark-green, inverted V-shaped roof. Presto: Ringer's Farmers Market was born!

What first struck me was all the government red tape I had to deal with just to operate a little business for a few months during the summer—paperwork for access to running water, a business license, a building permit, and more. I remember wondering who all those busybodies (i.e., bureaucrats) were who were getting in my way, impeding my progress, and costing me money before I even had the opportunity to open my doors. Why were they bothering me? Didn't they have anything better to do?

But what I remember most about that summer was working eighteen- to twenty-hour days, much of the time in the sweltering summer heat. I would get out of bed every morning between 2:00 and 4:00 a.m. and go down to the central market to buy my produce for the day. I quickly learned that the earlier I arrived at the central market, the better my chances of getting the best quality.

I also quickly learned how a true marketplace works, with prices being determined right out in the open through the unfiltered phenomenon of supply and demand. Farmers would bring their produce to the market in the wee hours, park their trucks, and display their fruits and vegetables for the army of wholesale buyers who, like me, were looking to acquire the best quality at the lowest possible prices.

It didn't take long for me to discover that if I bought high-quality produce at reasonable prices, I could make money. On the other hand, if I made the mistake of buying produce that was too ripe or too expensive, I could get burned and end up with a lot of unsalable inventory at the end of the day.

Despite my total lack of experience, I did quite well—and when I went back to school that fall, not only did I have some profit to show for my efforts, but I immediately started thinking about opening several produce stands the following year.

In the spring, I began scouting for good locations around town and going through the annoying process of talking to the government protection-racket guys about what I had to do to gain their permission to operate.

Then, as summer drew near, I hired college kids to work the seven red and green produce shacks that I'd had a carpenter build to my crude specs, bought an old truck to deliver inventory to each one, and paid all my licensing fees. Now I was a *real* Entrepreneur—putting everything on the line, but with a recklessness that comes only with youthful exuberance.

Every morning I would haul myself out of bed in the dark and drive to the central market to buy enough fruit and vegetables for my seven locations. Without stopping for breakfast, I would make the rounds in my shaky truck, dropping off each stand's allotment of produce for the day. Then I'd make the rounds several more times throughout the day, making sure that the produce was properly displayed and solving any problems that arose.

Since I was open seven days a week, the work was virtually nonstop. But even at that early stage of my business career, I realized that you have to be prepared to do whatever it takes.

As you might have guessed, I learned another lesson that summer: Rapid expansion and undercapitalization are a lethal mixture for an Entrepreneur. After making a good living from one produce stand the first summer, I ended up losing what was for me, at the time, a lot of money the following summer when I expanded to seven locations.

The multiplication (7 x 1 = 7) didn't work out in dollars and cents as it was supposed to. I discovered that increasing the size of an operation doesn't automatically increase profitability even if it increases sales. In my case, it was the additional costs of buying a truck and paying all those salaries that did me in. That's when I realized that the downside for every entrepreneurial project can be zero . . . or worse.

While I wound up with nothing, the kids who worked for me went back to school not only with extra money in their pockets but with the satisfaction of having had an enjoyable summer. I understood then why so many people choose to work fixed hours and draw a paycheck. But I recognized, too, that had my premature expansion plans been successful, I could have made a lot of money.

I witnessed, firsthand, Adam Smith's "invisible hand" at work in my little operation. I also saw that I had done far more than provide employment for some college kids. My customers loved my quality, service, and prices, so they, too, came out ahead *so long as I was making money.* But when I stopped making money, everyone—not just me, but my employees, customers, and suppliers—lost. It was crystal clear to me that my success was good for many other people and that, by contrast, my failure was bad for them.

I remember feeling satisfaction, despite the unpleasant financial outcome. It didn't occur to me that there were people in the world who might actually view me as a villain for my efforts to make a lot of money.

Entrepreneurship, the Advanced Course

I tried my hand at a number of other entrepreneurial pursuits in those early days, with varying degrees of success and failure. But the one common denominator was my willingness to do whatever I thought it would take to succeed.

It was during this period that politicians and liberals began to annoy me no end. It was clear to me that they believed others had a legitimate right to the fruits of my labor, yet it was also clear that they had absolutely no idea—nor did they care—how hard I worked for my money.

Nevertheless, the entrepreneurial attitude of doing whatever it takes to succeed was already deeply ingrained in my psyche. This was critically important many years later when I became an author and my first book was rejected by twenty-three publishers. I licked my prideful wounds and, without knowing anything about the publishing business, decided to publish the book myself.

Without exception, people who knew me thought I was out of my mind. Some even chastised me for having the audacity to believe I could publish a book that would have any chance of competing with the forty thousand books a year that were being published.

Since I had very little money to invest in this venture, I produced the first copies of my book in bound manuscript form, with a hardcover casing that I applied with an ancient Velobind machine. To market them, I ran inexpensive ads in local newspapers . . . with disastrous results. As my meager resources dwindled, I struggled to suppress the doubts that crept into my mind. But I didn't give up.

I found a way to meet with, and get advice from, the legendary Joe Karbo (as mentioned earlier, the author of *The Lazy Man's Way to Riches*). I also devoured David Ogilvy's *Confessions of an Advertising Man* and Claude Hopkins's classic *Scientific Advertising*. As a result, I learned how to write some pretty good ad copy and the book started to sell.

Just as young Jeff Bezos would do years later when he started Amazon.com, I personally wrapped each book I sold and took it to the post office. I did *whatever it took* to keep the project moving forward.

Eventually, I began writing full-page ads for my book and placing them in the *Wall Street Journal*. It was two years before I finally got B. Dalton, Waldenbooks, and a number of smaller bookstore chains to buy the book, but once they did, it really took off.

Within six months, it made the *New York Times* bestseller list, and about six months after that, it made it to number one. That ultimately led to my career as a bestselling author, which—as with my young-and-dumb days as a produce magnate—resulted in jobs for a lot of people.

It also resulted in a lot of profits for publishers, typesetters, printers, advertisers, public-relations firms, and others—and increased employment in those areas as well. There it was again, the ever-present invisible hand of the marketplace that waits patiently for the Entrepreneur who is willing to do whatever it takes to succeed.

The Big Two

My early days as an author exemplify two entrepreneurial traits that are essential to success: self-discipline and relentlessness.

If you aspire to be a writer, you can talk endlessly about your grandiose plans for writing a book, you can jabber about possible titles with your friends, and you can spend entire days thinking about what you want to write about. But, sooner or later, you have to come to grips with the reality that a writer is someone who writes—not now and then, not when he happens to feel like it, but *every day*. No excuses.

It isn't easy by any means. (As the late and legendary sportswriter Red Smith put it, "There is nothing to writing. All you do is sit down at a typewriter and open a vein.") It requires restraining, or regulating, your actions—repressing the instinct to act impulsively in favor of taking a rational, long-term approach. The serious Entrepreneur, like the serious writer, does not kid himself about this. He realizes that he *always* has a choice.

In this regard, I am reminded of Al Pacino's words in his Oscar-winning performance in *Scent of a Woman*. In a regretful tone, Pacino (playing the role of retired lieutenant colonel Frank Slade, a hell-raising ex-military officer) says, "I always knew what the right path was. Without exception, I knew. But I never took it. You know why? It was too damn hard."

To the Entrepreneur, *nothing* is "too damn hard." He knows that just because something is hard doesn't mean it's impossible. The Retrogressive, on the other hand, is inclined to believe that success is impossible for the average person, which is why benevolent government must help him.

The Retrogressive sees no reason for the Entrepreneur to be rewarded in the marketplace simply because he is self-disciplined and relentless. In fact, he believes the Entrepreneur should share his earnings with someone who is not fortunate enough to possess these qualities. The possibility that every normal human being has the capacity to *develop* these traits is unthinkable to him, because it doesn't fit in with his fixed-pie view of the world.

Another Whatever-It-Takes Awakening

In the early 1980s, my entrepreneurial instincts drew me into the emerging cellular-telephone industry. I became involved with an attorney who had developed an assembly-line approach for filing applications for cellular licenses in markets throughout the country. One of the most interesting things that came out of this relationship was that he introduced me to a young man ("Bruce") whom he had been talking to about how they might work together.

Bruce was a bespectacled African-American who was obviously extremely bright and entrepreneurial to the core. His office, a single, large room, was filled with a handful of men and women, all of whom looked to be in their twenties, energetically working at computers and other hi-tech equipment.

After Bruce had shown me around and explained a bit about his operation, I made an off-the-cuff remark to the effect of "You guys look like you're really serious here. I'm impressed that you're working on Saturday." To which he replied, "Saturday? Are you kidding? We work seven days and seven nights a week here. We worked on Thanksgiving. We worked on Christmas. We worked on New Year's Day. Everyone here understood what the ground rules were before they became involved."

He went on to say, "The cellular-telephone window that's been opened by the FCC is a once-in-a-lifetime opportunity, and it's not going to stay open forever. My dad once told me that when the door opens for you, make it clear to everyone that they need to get out of your way, then do whatever you have to do to go through it. There are billions of dollars at stake here, and I couldn't live with myself if I didn't do whatever it takes to get a big chunk of that money."

I never forgot those words. I've probably quoted them a hundred times over the years. I have no idea how much money Bruce ended up making in the cellular-telephone lotteries that ensued, but I'd be surprised if he didn't become very wealthy.

While millions of folks are enjoying the artificial-prosperity good life—including millions of Retrogressives who sincerely believe that capitalism is evil—there are millions of Entrepreneurs like Bruce who are working away quietly and relentlessly in their one-room offices . . . their basements . . . their attics . . . their garages . . . committed to doing whatever it takes to build a better mousetrap and become rich in the process.

It's a hard pill for the Retrogressive to swallow, but, thanks yet again to the invisible hand of the marketplace, the Entrepreneur who works while others play—not to make everyone else's life better but to make his *own* life better—makes the world a better place for others as an unintended consequence.

This is an entrepreneurial fact of life that is incomprehensible to the union automaton who lives by the whistle—the whistle that tells him it's time for his morning coffee break, the whistle that tells him it's time for lunch, the whistle that tells him it's time for his afternoon coffee break, the whistle that tells him it's time to quit and go home because he's done all his work for the day.

The fact is, no one ever does *all* of his work—regardless of his profession—because that would imply that he's done everything he could possibly do to succeed. The Entrepreneur knows that his work is never done. Every day that he works while others play is one additional day that he moves ahead of his competition.

I remember when, years ago, the prolific Gary North wrote that he loved Yom Kippur because it gave him a one-day advantage over his Jewish friends who took the day off to worship. Harsh but humorous. And if you know Gary North, you have no doubt that he really meant what he said. Just the thought is enough to give a Retrogressive hives.

The Silver Spoon That Wasn't

Another milestone for me in cementing the "whatever-it-takes" mantra of the successful Entrepreneur in my brain came when I read the book *Hard Drive* in the early nineties. It's a detailed account of Bill Gates's life and how he built the Microsoft empire—and it's full of surprises.

For one thing, it's widely believed that Gates grew up with a silver spoon in his mouth, and to some extent that's true. After all, his father was a prominent attorney. But somewhere in Bill Gates's DNA was a superentrepreneurial gene.

When, for example, he was just thirteen years old and in the eighth grade, he and some of his nerdy little friends (including his future Microsoft partner Paul Allen) made a deal to get free computer time from Computer Center Corporation ("C-Cubed") in exchange for trying to create "bugs" that would crash the company's system. They worked at nights and on weekends, when paying customers were not likely to be logged on.

After dinner each evening, Gates would jump on a bus and rush over to C-Cubed, work past midnight, then usually walk home. Allen would sometimes hoist Gates up so he could search for information in trash cans left behind by the day shift at C-Cubed.[1]

The idea that someone would want to work while others are blissfully sleeping or having a good time is anathema to the Retrogressive. In his morally superior view of the way the world should function, the Retrogressive demands that a Bill Gates share his wealth with those less fortunate than he—which makes me want to ask what, exactly, he means by "less fortunate." Less fortunate because they didn't have the ambition to work until the wee hours of the morning when they were thirteen years old? Less fortunate because they weren't willing to work nights, weekends, and holidays? Less fortunate because they weren't willing to do whatever it took to succeed?

My question, of course, would be of no interest to the Retrogressive. All that's important to him is that the "fortunate" share their wealth with the "less fortunate."

Gates's willingness to do whatever it took to succeed became more and more apparent once he was in business for himself. Some years after he brought in his old college buddy Steve Ballmer as his assistant in 1980, Gates said in an interview: "When we got up to thirty [employees], it was still just me, a secretary, and twenty-eight programmers. I wrote all the checks, answered the mail, took the phone calls."[2]

Imagine, Gates had thirty employees and was still writing the checks, handling the mail, and answering the phone.

The average person who moans and groans about his job has no idea that he can probably handle a much bigger workload—make that *much* bigger—than the one he's complaining about. Nevertheless, the Retrogressive insists that the Entrepreneur should give up some of the pie he voluntarily works so hard to bake. How absurd.

Gates didn't trample on others and grab an inordinately big slice of an imaginary community pie to get ahead. He baked his own pie! He created wealth—and made millions of others wealthy in the process. In addition, as a result of his efforts, he changed the lives of billions of people throughout the world for the better and, as is so often the case with megasuccessful entrepreneurs, after Gates accumulated his fortune, he ended up being one of the greatest philanthropists of our time. But that was by choice. Being charitable, yes; taking the property of others by force, no. (More on charity in a later chapter.)

Bill Gates's story magnifies the reality that his obsession to do whatever it took to succeed improved the lives of untold numbers of people whom he would never even meet. Nevertheless, the Retrogressive is blind to such invisible benefits, which is why he believes that government has a moral duty to force those it deems to be rich to share the fruits of their labor with those it deems to be in need.

I can just imagine some readers thinking to themselves, "But what's so noble about working all the time and spending less time with your family?" I didn't say it was noble. It's just what the ambitious Entrepreneur chooses to do.

There is no doubt that the Entrepreneur faces a tough

challenge trying to be a good spouse and parent while also being relentlessly focused on his work. But guess what? That's *his* problem—and no one else's business. The individual who chooses to spend more time with his family rather than working is neither morally superior nor inferior to the individual who chooses the opposite path. The fact is that how hard one chooses to work has nothing whatsoever to do with morality. It's simply a lifestyle choice.

Life is full of choices, and in a free society, your choices are none of my business and my choices are none of your business. I have no claim to any part of your earnings, and you have no claim to any part of my earnings.

Having said this, I would still argue that the Entrepreneur who makes the choice to do whatever it takes to succeed is a hero, because he shoulders a much greater burden than the average person when it comes to stimulating economic growth and creating jobs—not to mention the products and services he provides that enrich the lives of others. To revile him for his efforts is to exhibit a Retrogressive psychosis that is harmful to a nation's financial health.

Follow-through

When, during the Tampa Bay Buccaneers' record twenty-six-game losing streak, a reporter asked Coach John McKay what he thought of his team's execution, McKay said, with a straight face, "I think it's a good idea."

I've never suffered through twenty-six straight losses at anything, but I must admit that I have long favored execution for those who fail to execute. For the Entrepreneur, the most unpleasant aspect of daily business is dealing with people who act as though they're sleepwalking.

I never cease to be amazed by people who repeatedly make adamant promises, then fail to follow through. I've grown weary of listening to those who always speak in the future tense, saying that they're *going* to take care of this or that tomorrow. As one tomorrow rolls into the next, my trust in these folks declines at an accelerating rate.

In Chapter 1, I mentioned Stephen M. R. Covey's book *The Speed of Trust,* in which Covey makes the case that, in the world of business, trust makes everything go faster. Covey also points out that trust is based not only on character but on competence—most commonly manifested in results. It's possible to trust someone's honesty but not trust him to deliver results—just as it's possible to trust someone to deliver results but not trust his honesty. Either way, dealing with such people slows you down.

For the Entrepreneur, following through to completion is an essential aspect of doing whatever it takes to succeed. Double-checking and triple-checking to get the results he's after are his trademarks.

People who can't comprehend double- and triple-checking often get in a huff when they are called to task for something that is incorrect. Their attitude is: "How many times do I have to do this !%*!# thing?" The answer, of course, is: "Until you get it right!"

The Entrepreneur never uses the excuse that he's too tired or, worse, too busy to check his work. He knows that people who are counting on him to deliver results don't have a great deal of interest in how tired or how busy he is. What they are interested in is his following through and giving them what he promised, giving it to them correctly, and giving it to them on time.

Overcoming Obstacles

When my wife and I were checking out high schools for our son, prominently displayed in the main hallway of one of the schools we visited was a large sign that read: "Life's Rational Rules of the World." There were twelve rules listed in all, and the first one read: "The world is not always fair."

Painful, but true. One of the few guarantees parents can make to their children with absolute confidence is that throughout their lives they will continually be confronted by injustice. The Entrepreneur understands this truism, both intellectually and emotionally, and realizes that (1) the more he focuses on the adversity in his life, the more adversity he is likely to face, and (2) the more he focuses on solutions, the more likely he is to overcome adversity.

The Retrogressive, on the other hand, thinks to himself, "Life isn't fair (by my standards), and I am therefore obliged to change the way life works." Hey, if life were fair, there would be no such thing as a Retrogressive in the first place. In fact, there would be no such thing as government;

everyone would simply govern himself. But the Entrepreneur, knowing that he must operate in the real world, accepts the reality that the world isn't always fair and moves forward with his life.

There are an infinite number of "unfair" obstacles that an Entrepreneur may have to overcome throughout his career, but there are two, in particular, that I want to mention here.

Handicaps

As a result of contracting scarlet fever, Thomas Edison became deaf at the age of fourteen. Throughout the rest of his life, he was completely deaf in his left ear and 80 percent deaf in his right ear. In spite of his handicap, he created products that have given millions of people better lives.

And Edison is but one of thousands of remarkable Entrepreneurs who managed to rise above their physical handicaps and make giant contributions to society. My favorite story in this regard is that of my longtime friend Jim Blanchard, perhaps because I was able to witness his amazing entrepreneurial accomplishments at close range.

Jim was an early Ayn Rand devotee, and an outspoken opponent of the welfare state. He believed in individualism at an age when most kids don't even know what the word means.

One evening during his senior year in high school, after

drinking heavily at a dance, he and two of his buddies made the mistake of deciding to drive home. It was raining heavily, and people rarely wore seatbelts in those days.

The guy who was behind the wheel did what teenagers usually do when they're drunk: He drove much too fast. Flying down St. Charles Avenue at seventy miles an hour, he failed to negotiate a curve in the road. The car flew up in the air and slammed into an oak tree. Jim, who had been in the backseat of the car, was catapulted through the air like a human cannonball. His flight came to an abrupt halt when his body hit a light pole. In that instant, at the tender age of seventeen, Jim's life was forever changed.

He vividly recalled a priest giving him his last rites at the scene of the accident, but that proved to be premature. Jim woke up in Charity Hospital with no feeling in either of his legs. An intern broke the news to him that his spinal cord had been severed in three places and that he would never walk again.

When Jim finally came home, his doting parents wanted to do everything possible for him. Though he loved his parents dearly, their over-protectiveness made him uncomfortable.

He had heard about a program in Mexico where paraplegics and quadriplegics lived together and learned to become self-sufficient. After doing some investigating, he made the decision to go there and begin the long process of turning his life around.

He spent five months in Mexico, and after he returned

home he finished his senior year of high school. He then earned a college degree and went on to become a remarkable Entrepreneur, building one hugely successful company after another. In 1971, he invested fifty dollars in a coin business, built it into a huge success, and ultimately sold it to General Electric Capital Corporation for enough millions to make him independently wealthy for life.

When an indescribably painful event intervenes in a person's life, as it did in Jim Blanchard's, he has two choices: He can feel sorry for himself and give up, or he can pick himself up, brush himself off, and move forward with increased determination.

Inspirational stories like Jim's abound in the entrepreneurial world. And it's not just physical handicaps that can challenge the Entrepreneur. A person with attention-deficit disorder has a handicap; a person with a low IQ has a handicap; a person with a lack of higher education has a handicap; a person who was abused as a child has a handicap; a person who comes from a poverty-stricken family has a handicap.

The truth be known, everyone has at least one handicap—and usually many. No one—including some of the most successful Entrepreneurs on earth—makes it through life without having to deal with a handicap that makes achievement more difficult.

It's not always possible for a person to overcome his handicaps, but it *is* possible for him to succeed *in spite of* his handicaps. The Entrepreneur gets it; the Retrogressive does not.

Negativism

Negativism stalks the Entrepreneur wherever he goes. Whether it's Thomas Edison's ten thousand failed attempts to invent the light bulb, Colonel Sanders's one thousand rejections of his fried chicken recipe, or Tommy Hilfiger's two failed ventures before his comeback to become a household name in men's and women's fashion, the Entrepreneur must have the self-confidence to rise above the derision and ridicule of his critics and keep moving forward.

Richard Branson became a billionaire by stubbornly moving ahead with entrepreneurial pursuits that even his closest advisors insisted would not work. "That's outdated" . . . "It's been tried before" . . . "There's no market for it" . . . their negativity went on and on. Great Entrepreneurs develop the mental toughness to ignore such tripe.

How well I remember Wall Street's skepticism of Jeff Bezos's brainchild, Amazon.com, when the company failed to make a profit during its first six years of operation, not to mention the widespread criticism of Google in its early years. Many pundits predicted Google would go out of business because it had no visible strategy for monetizing its search-engine technology.

Rest assured that there are young Entrepreneurs like Google's Larry Page and Sergey Brin working away right now in their basements and plotting to overtake Google. This kind of whatever-it-takes entrepreneurial spirit is precisely what stimulates a nation's economy and what built America into the most powerful economic force on earth.

With self-discipline, persistence, and resourcefulness, Walt Disney and a mouse transformed the amusement-park concept into the world's largest shopping mall. Ray Kroc transformed the hamburger stand into the fast-food industry. Wolfgang Puck transformed the gourmet-chef profession into the gourmet-chef conglomerate.

One of my favorite success stories about rising above negativism is how Bill Rasmussen and his son Scott transformed the concept of sports on television by starting ESPN. Rasmussen had been an announcer for the Hartford Whalers for four years, when, in the 1977–78 season, the team missed the playoffs for the first time ever. In crisis-shakeup mode, management fired nearly everyone, including Rasmussen. It turned out to be a blessing in disguise, because it forced him to look for an offsetting opportunity.

The idea he came up with was ESPN, but Rasmussen said that everyone in the television industry—without a single exception—told him that his brainchild had absolutely no chance of succeeding.

In a bold entrepreneurial move, Rasmussen implemented his plan anyway, and ESPN became an overnight success. An interesting side note to this story is that not only did Rasmussen overcome the negativity of his critics, he also demonstrated how the Entrepreneur is able to turn adversity into success. Rasmussen has often said that if he had not been fired by the Hartford Whalers, ESPN never would have been born.

When you think about how much entertainment ESPN has provided for millions of viewers—not to mention the tens of thousands of jobs it has created through the years— the government should give Bill and Scott Rasmussen a 100 percent tax break for life. Share their wealth? Why? They've already contributed more than their share to the rest of society—and, yes, they've done so at a profit.

Because the Entrepreneur's success creates jobs, stimulates the economy, and results in better products and services at lower prices for everyone, he is a hero in every sense of the word. Instead of recognizing this, the Retrogressive focuses on the "unfairness" of people having to work "too many" hours under conditions that he considers to be inhumane. He continually tries to stifle the Entrepreneur's efforts by appealing to the government to institute legislation that kills jobs and destroys the economy. As a result, he creates shortages and causes prices to increase.

The Retrogressive's belief that everyone should be rewarded just for being alive may sound great to some people, but, in actual practice, it is a philosophy of destruction. When you try to equalize results, what you end up with is equal slaves.

Above all, the Retrogressive is contemptuous of the Entrepreneur's willingness to do whatever it takes to succeed.

Far from viewing him as a hero, the Retrogressive sees the Entrepreneur as a greedy exploiter of his fellow man. Which is why I said earlier that to believe there can be a compromise between these two fundamentally different points of view is naïve to an extreme. Progress and retrogression are mutually exclusive objectives.

4.

The Foundation for Entrepreneurship

The U.S. Chamber of Commerce mission statement is a perfect description of the philosophy upon which entrepreneurship is based: "To advance human progress through an economic, political, and social system based on individual freedom, incentive, initiative, opportunity, and responsibility." Note that neither the words *free enterprise* nor *capitalism* are used in this mission statement, which, at first blush, may seem odd. Throughout this book, I use these terms interchangeably, so you may consider their definitions to be combined whenever I allude to either of them. Individually, however, they are defined as follows:

Capitalism: *an economic system in which investment in and ownership of the means of production, distribution, and exchange of wealth is made and maintained chiefly by private individuals or corporations, especially as contrasted to cooperatively or state-owned means of wealth production.*

It is important to understand that capitalism is not a system unto itself. It is simply a subcategory of a broader philosophy—the philosophy of freedom, which encompasses, among other things, social and economic interactions. If people are truly free, then, by definition, they must be able to operate in a free-market economy.

Capitalism is the freedom to trade goods, services, and labor freely with other people and companies. True capitalism is unfettered and unregulated, which means that people

81

are free to buy and sell whatever they please to anyone who, without being coerced, is willing to deal with them.

Free enterprise: *an economic and political doctrine holding that a capitalist economy can regulate itself in a freely competitive market through the relationship of supply and demand, with a minimum of governmental intervention and regulation.*

In other words, contrary to the Retrogressive's belief that the government must regulate "greedy" Entrepreneurs, the market, through the law of supply and demand, is an infinitely more effective (and just) regulator than all of the politicians in the world combined. In fact, it would be accurate to say that the market is never wrong. Why? Because it always rewards those who produce products and services at prices people are willing to pay and punishes those who do not.

The free market is a giant hodgepodge of goods, services, labor, and capital coming together naturally and mixing with the unique wants, needs, desires, personality, and financial situation of each consumer. In other words, it is not a collective concept. On the contrary, it's all about the individual and his desire to better *his* existence.

Freedom is the ideal environment for the Entrepreneur, because the more free he is, the more creative he can be, the more actions he can take, the more opportunity he has to become financially successful, the more quickly he can expand his business, the more jobs he can create (as a necessary side effect), and the more he stimulates the economy (again, as a side effect of his efforts).

It's breathtaking to imagine what the Entrepreneur would be able to accomplish without government intervention. In a true laissez-faire economy—which, by the way, has never existed on this planet—the Entrepreneur would be able to create wealth on a scale that is impossible for the Retrogressive to comprehend.

The closest mankind has come to reaching the ideal of totally unfettered financial freedom was in the United States during roughly its first century-and-a-half of existence and in Hong Kong before its being turned over to China. (In fairness to China, I should point out that its ruling oligarchy has been pragmatic enough to leave most of Hong Kong's efficient capitalist structure in place. As a result, China has been able to support the artificially inflated U.S. economy by buying up America's debt instruments on a vast scale.)

While the dream of the Entrepreneur is a laissez-faire capitalist society, the reality, even in the freest country in the world, is "state capitalism," which is now the norm in so-called industrialized societies. What differs from country to country is the *degree* of government involvement in the economy. China is the best—and most successful— example of state capitalism. It is on course to become the most powerful economy in the world over the next five years or so, with new Entrepreneur millionaires emerging in that country virtually every day, along with a rapidly growing middle class.

State capitalism, at its best, is akin to a benevolent dictatorship, and a benevolent dictatorship works for a majority of the people who live in such a society and play by the benevolent dictator's rules. The problem with state capitalism is that the government picks winners and losers in the marketplace. So if you're an Entrepreneur in a country such as China, your opportunity for success is very much dependent on how the controlling oligarchy feels about you. Worse, when the (so-called) benevolent ruler dies or is overthrown, the next guy in line to become dictator may be the ambitious Entrepreneur's worst nightmare.

Take Russia, for example. Boris Yeltsin is long gone and Mikhail Gorbachev is out of the picture. Suddenly, KGBer Vladimir Putin and his valet, Dmitry Medvedev, are in charge, and state capitalism is in full bloom. But as billionaire Mikhail Khodorkovsky discovered, you get to become a wealthy man in Russia, and continue to enjoy your wealth, only if you please the not-so-benevolent Putin. Step out of line, and you can quickly find yourself out of business—or in jail.

Even in the United States, government corrupts the marketplace by favoring some companies and individuals over others. Barack Obama's incestuous relationship with Jeffrey Immelt and General Electric is an extreme example of this.

Government is a never-ending threat to the Entrepreneur because it intervenes in the marketplace daily and, by so doing, violates his natural rights. The Founding Fathers repeatedly warned us to distrust the government, and ultimately drafted a Constitution for the *specific* purpose of protecting individuals and companies from its lust for power. The failure of Americans to heed the warnings of the Founding Fathers has brought the United States to the verge of financial collapse and possible dictatorship.

The Founders did not give the federal government the authority to "create jobs," "get the economy moving," or "strengthen the middle class." These are nothing more than Retrogressive euphemisms for increasing government power and crowding out Entrepreneurs who create real wealth, real jobs, and a fundamentally strong economy through the natural workings of the marketplace.

The belief that a president or Congress has the power to create private-sector jobs and legitimately stimulate the economy is ludicrous on its face, yet the vast majority of voters accept it as though it were a proven fact. The reason for this can be found in French philosopher Michel de Montaigne's observation that "Men are most apt to believe what they least understand." The vast majority of the population knows nothing about macroeconomics (and some would argue that the same is true of most professional economists), so they are ripe to believe almost anything—especially if it sounds like it's going to line their pockets.

In order for the Entrepreneur to work his wonders to the maximum, what he most needs from Washington is for government to step aside. The truth is that economic downturns are only prolonged by government intervention, because an important key to entrepreneurial growth of the economy is smaller, less intrusive government.

Contrary to what politicians keep telling us, a true Entrepreneur does not want Republicans and Democrats to "work together" to "get something done," because he knows that getting something done in Washington almost always means higher taxes, more regulations, and less freedom. Some of the most destructive legislation in this country's history has been "bipartisan."

Governor Bobby Jindal has it right when he says that we should have a part-time Congress, because the more Congress is in session, the worse off we are. Or, as Will Rogers put it, "It's a good thing we don't get all the government we pay for."

Greed

The Entrepreneur is often accused of being "greedy"—and, indeed, he is. Greed is, quite simply, the desire to acquire. And, though it may ruffle the feathers of the Retrogressive to hear it, the reality is that *all* human beings possess such a desire.

Normal people, however, realize that, due to limited time and resources, they must pick the things that are most important to them and be willing to let go of other desires that are of lesser importance. That doesn't mean they don't want the items they don't acquire. In fact, they may want them very badly. It just means that they want other items even more, and, thus, those are the ones they choose to buy.

But different people have different desires. One person might desire to acquire material wealth by providing

The Foundation for Entrepreneurship

products or services that people are willing to purchase from him. Another person might desire to acquire power over others by leading or joining a crusade of some kind. And still another individual might desire to acquire the respect of others through artistic achievements. Regardless of their objectives, all of these people are "greedy" in the sense that they "desire to acquire."

Though the audience was set up to hiss and boo when Gordon Gekko, in the 1987 movie *Wall Street,* spewed out those now-famous words "Greed is good," the fact is that greed is neither good nor bad; it's neutral. It is only the *methods* that a person employs to fulfill his desires (i.e., satisfy his "greed") that are good or bad.

Just as guns do not kill people, neither do greed or ambition, of and by themselves, harm anyone. So long as the Entrepreneur does not use force or fraud, he need not apologize for being "greedy"—and certainly not for any success he is able to achieve through raw ambition and hard work.

The Myth of the Zero-sum Game

A few years back, a *Time* magazine cover story on ambition stated, "Of all the impulses in humanity's behavioral portfolio, ambition—that need to grab an ever bigger piece of the resource pie before someone else gets it—ought to be one of the most democratically distributed. Nature is a zero-sum game, after all. Every buffalo you kill for your family is one less for somebody else's; every acre of land you occupy elbows out somebody else."[1]

This kind of Marxist rhetoric is precisely what deters the underprivileged from becoming entrepreneurial and lifting themselves up. Ignorant, left-wing professors have been teaching such gibberish to malleable-minded college kids for centuries, while at the same time shameless and/or guilt-ridden politicians have been brainwashing the parents of those same children.

Long before the White House brain trust reinvented Michelle Obama and created a let's-pretend project (the "anti–childhood obesity campaign") for Barack Obama's bitter half (credit, Michelle Malkin), she blurted out her now-famous hammer-and-sickle comment, "Someone is going to have to give up a piece of their pie so that someone else can have more." In politically incorrect circles, this is a euphemism for *communism*.

The idea of being forced to give up some of your pie assumes not only that the size of the pie is fixed, but that there is only one pie, which I like to affectionately refer to as *the Michelle Pie*. Attention mentally challenged Retrogressives: There is no limit to the number of pies that can be baked. The only way to stop the Entrepreneur from baking more pies is through force—usually government force. Lacking that, he will continue to bake pies that he believes people will like—and buy—and everyone will benefit from his "selfish" efforts.

Having said this, I feel obliged to once again emphasize that the purpose of a business is to make as much money as possible—not by dealing with others "fairly" (which is an abstract word trap), but, rather, without resorting to coercion, fraud, or aggression. Unfortunately, much of the coercion, fraud, and aggression that infest the marketplace—and thus make it *unfree*—has its roots in governmental mischief.

What the Retrogressive cannot seem to grasp is that when the Entrepreneur creates wealth for himself, he creates value for others in the process. Or, to continue the metaphor, he increases the size of the pie. That's why the poorest families in the United States have the means to buy state-of-the-art television sets, DVD players, video-game consoles, computers, cell phones, and an endless array of other electronic gadgets that are not necessities by any stretch of the imagination.

Again, capitalism is but one aspect of freedom—the freedom to achieve financial success without government interference. It is the ideal foundation for entrepreneurship, and thus for creating a strong economy. But notwithstanding the merits of capitalism, there are some capitalists who try to find ways to achieve profits through fraudulent actions.

Earlier, I said the same thing about Entrepreneurs. Not all Entrepreneurs are honest, but that does not take away from the fact that entrepreneurship is a noble activity when practiced by honest Entrepreneurs. (To make a distinction between Entrepreneurs and capitalists, I guess you could say that all Entrepreneurs are capitalists, but not all capitalists are Entrepreneurs.) There are Entrepreneurs who are dishonest, just as there are workers who are dishonest. There are priests who are dishonest, and, yes, there are even politicians who are dishonest. I know, I know . . . a dishonest politician is hard to imagine, but they do exist. The point is that there are people in every field of endeavor who are dishonest.

President Herbert Hoover is purported to have said that the only thing wrong with capitalism is capitalists. And he was right. Capitalism is freedom in its purest form. Problems arise only when some capitalists use that freedom to defraud or cheat others. Hoover could just as well have said that the only thing wrong with humanitarianism is humans, and he would have been right about that as well. Which is why the notion that all capitalists are evil people who exploit the masses is a ridiculous and totally unsubstantiated generalization.

Fortunately, we have a legal system that punishes criminal Entrepreneurs and capitalists. Just ask Ivan Boesky, Dennis Kozlowski, Charles Keating, Bernie Madoff, et al. Sure, some criminal Entrepreneurs and capitalists manage to beat the system and escape punishment, but that's also true of countless murderers, rapists, arsonists, bank robbers, priests, and, above all, politicians. (Isn't it remarkable that people like Barney Frank, Charles Schumer, Nancy Pelosi, and Harry Reid are not behind bars?)

Exceptions aside, capitalism is the most moral economic system ever conceived. Nevertheless, the Retrogressive loves to paint those who believe in capitalism as greedy, selfish, and ruthless. And because we live in a

country moving rapidly from soft socialism to hard socialism, advocating a laissez-faire capitalistic society is considered extreme. (The ultimate perversion is that even though
all redistribution-of-wealth programs are both unconstitutional and immoral, those who advocate more of such
programs are not considered extreme or immoral.)

After more than a hundred years of moving America
toward socialism, Retrogressives now take the position
that all of the unconstitutional legislation they have passed
over the last century is the norm—the "baseline," as it
were. Unfortunately, they're right. Remember, communism was the norm in the Soviet Union for seventy years.
So when Mikhail Gorbachev implemented *perestroika* (the
restructuring of the country's political and economic system) and *glasnost* (essentially, freedom of the press), those
measures were viewed by the Communist Party establishment as extreme.

But one man's extremist is another man's liberator. No
one ever put it better than Barry Goldwater when he said,
in his acceptance speech as the 1964 Republican presidential candidate, "I would remind you that extremism in the
defense of liberty is no vice! And let me remind you also
that moderation in the pursuit of justice is no virtue!"

I remember how horrified many people were by Goldwater's words. He was considered an extremist by a majority of voters—which amazed me, because I couldn't
understand how anyone could possibly *not* believe that
being extreme on the subjects of liberty and justice was a
good thing.

Goldwater, a courageous man who did not back down from his beliefs, was a half century ahead of his time. In his 1960 book *The Conscience of a Conservative,* he was right in synch with today's Tea Party movement.

I have little interest in streamlining government or in making it more efficient, for I mean to reduce its size. I do not undertake to promote welfare, for I propose to extend freedom. My aim is not to pass laws, but to repeal them. It is not to inaugurate new programs, but to cancel old ones that do violence to the Constitution, or that have failed their purpose, or that impose on the people an unwarranted financial burden. I will not attempt to discover whether legislation is "needed" before I have first determined whether it is constitutionally permissible. And if I should later be attacked for neglecting my constituents' "interests," I shall reply that I was informed that their main interest is liberty and that in that cause I am doing the very best I can.[2]

All those Republicans who are dodging and twisting and turning to avoid questions about such issues as privatizing Social Security, phasing out Medicare, eliminating the minimum wage, and getting rid of such redistribution-of-wealth programs as unemployment benefits and food stamps should read and reread Goldwater's words. For a modern-day example, they need only follow the lead of Ron Paul, who looks at all legislation from two aspects: (1) Is it constitutional? and (2) Can we afford it? And in the vast majority of cases, the answer to both questions is *no*.

As any fool knows, nothing in life is free. The only way government can give people *free* anything is to violate the *freedom* of those who pay for it. Yet, it is considered by many media pundits and politicians to be extreme whenever someone suggests cutting a welfare program.

By today's standards, that would make the Founding Fathers extremists. And they were. They were, in fact, extreme when it came to the issue of human freedom. After all, there isn't a single provision in the Constitution for the government to fulfill the needs and desires of individual citizens. Meanwhile, because capitalism is *not* a zero-sum game, entrepreneurship has done more to fulfill the needs and desires of people throughout the world than the efforts of all governments combined.

Competition and the Marketplace

In a capitalistic society, a person has a right to be lazy. But under true laissez-faire capitalism, laziness would be the exception, because the marketplace doesn't reward laziness. The marketplace rewards those who produce products and services that people want.

This can be frustrating for the average hardworking individual. Even I scratch my head in wonderment whenever

I hear about a professional athlete signing a $100 million contract. Imagine never having to do any real work as an adult and living like royalty just because you were born with great athletic skills. But in a free market, just as it's okay to be lazy, it's also okay to be lucky. People win lotteries all the time. Hey, look at the lottery Melinda Gates won just by being in the right place at the right time to become Mrs. Bill Gates.

Then there are the actors who get paid small fortunes in a strange profession that pays you to pretend that you're someone else. Is that fair? If you believe in freedom, then, yes, it's fair. I think Rush Limbaugh said it best when Chris Wallace asked him, with regard to his purported $400 million radio contract, how anyone could possibly be worth that much money. Without hesitation, Limbaugh answered, "Because that's what people are willing to pay me."

That is what capitalism is all about—what consumers are willing to pay for what they want to buy, not what politicians and government bureaucrats *think* they should buy and *think* they should pay. It's also why capitalism is the eternal enemy of the Retrogressive. If people are free to buy what they want from whomever they want, it prevents the Retrogressive from using what he believes to be his superior intellect to make those decisions for them. The fact is that people's choices about their purchases are nobody else's business—including and especially the government's.

Another important aspect of capitalism is that it weeds out inefficient, outdated businesses, which makes room for efficient, modern enterprises. And it is the Entrepreneur who keeps this natural process moving forward by constantly coming up with better, more useful, less expensive products.

The Entrepreneur is forever on the lookout for opportunity in the form of an underserved market—and competition only fuels his fire. For example:

- In 1980, the major television networks were caught off guard by Ted Turner when he placed a bet on his vision of the future and created an upstart cable-television station called CNN. And sixteen years later, Rupert Murdoch, a transplanted Australian Entrepreneur, saw the liberal bias in the media and bet millions that viewers would flock to hear the news from a conservative point of view.

  Once Fox News was launched, it didn't take the world long to realize a heretofore well-hidden fact: Most Americans have conservative values. This was a dagger in the hearts of Retrogressive news commentators who had become used to creating their own news by leaving out pertinent facts and knowingly adding false information—and, often, by simply ignoring news items that didn't fit their liberal agenda.

  Without government intervention—like that proposed by FCC "Chief Diversity Officer" Mark Lloyd—it's hard to imagine how CNN, CNBC, and MSNBC can continue in business much longer. Even the three major networks are getting clobbered, yet they cling to their left-wing agendas, choosing to ignore the desires of a majority of American viewers and voters while the marketplace continues to destroy them.

- Pay phones (remember them?) gave way to cell phones. You can probably recall when owning a cell phone was like carrying around a brick all day. This wasn't fifty years ago; it was the mid-eighties! Today, the smallest cell phone can fit in your shirt pocket. Not only has cell-phone size and versatility changed, so has our reliance on cellular service. Nearly 10 percent of U.S. households that have cellular phones no longer have landline service. Talk about change. There was a time when you couldn't even sign up for cellular service if you didn't have a home telephone number.

    I was involved in the early days of cellular telephone, so I'm well aware of the moneymaking opportunities that were created by Entrepreneurs who predicted the future of a technology that few people had even heard of when I wrote my first article about it in 1982.

- In 1995, a kid named Jeff Bezos, betting that the future of the retail book business would be on the Internet, put his idea into action, called it

Amazon.com, and ended up dictating the business strategy of giants like Borders (now deceased, thanks to marketplace destruction) and Barnes & Noble for years to come.

- A few years later, two kids named Sergey Brin and Larry Page started a little search-engine company called Google, which became the first serious challenger to Microsoft's overall dominance. Their foresight changed the world as we once knew it. (Given recent events that appear to tie Google to Retrogressive government, however, perhaps it's not the kind of change we want.)

YouTube . . . Facebook . . . Twitter . . . what's next? Things change, and sharp Entrepreneurs have a knack for predicting what those changes will be—then putting everything on the line to back up their predictions. In a true laissez-faire market, entrepreneurial creativity would explode, and real wealth would increase dramatically for those who were willing to compete for it. A free market is wide open to competition, and competition is the consumer's best friend.

Does Size Matter?

One of the many problems the Retrogressive has with capitalism is that he believes the little guy can't compete with giant firms because the deck is stacked against him. Nothing could be further from the truth. In a free market, size matters, but it doesn't carry the day. What matters more are creativity, persistence, and, above all, resourcefulness.

People often marvel at how Walmart snuck up on Sears, which was the largest retailer in the world for decades. In the beginning, Walmart was a joke in retailing circles—a small regional company with stores in towns that had populations of five thousand or less. The fat-cat Sears board members and top executives, up to their ears in perks and golden parachutes, never even saw Sam Walton coming.

Sears thought it was being prudent by keeping one eye on Target and the other on Kmart. Too bad it didn't have a third eye in the back of its corporate head to keep tabs on that little retailer from Bentonville, Arkansas.

Yes, size matters, but it doesn't insulate one from failure. Just think of the poor elephant. He's the largest land animal on the planet, but that hasn't done him a whole lot of good. In fact, his main problem is that he's *too* big. Just to absorb all the oxygen he requires, he needs an acre of lung surface. He has to roam around sixteen hours each and every day to find hundreds of pounds of grass and foliage to satisfy his hundreds of feet of intestines and complex digestive organs. Worse, because of his enormous size, he can't even jump over a seven-foot trench.[3]

I tell you, size is overrated—which is why the true Entrepreneur does not fear major corporations. Upstart Microsoft didn't fear giant IBM, upstart Google didn't fear giant Microsoft, and some upstart Entrepreneur who is working away in his garage at this very moment doesn't fear giant Google. The start-up Entrepreneur has many advantages over the big guys, one of the most important being that he can move much more swiftly and nimbly than elephants like IBM, Microsoft, and Google.

Supply and Demand—the Free Market in Action

A couple of years ago, a series of snowstorms blasted the Middle Atlantic states and the East Coast. When the first big snowfall hit, I pictured being socked in for a week or more, so I was a good prospect for someone willing to do the hard labor of removing snow from my driveway.

As luck would have it, I spotted a fellow with a snow blower removing the snow from our neighbor's driveway. I asked him if he would like to shovel our driveway as well, and, if so, how much he would charge. He quoted me $100, which seemed kind of high, but I wasn't about to let him slip away.

He had the supply, and the demand on my end was high. So a hundred bucks it was. No government involvement, no regulations, no price controls. Best of all, I think it's safe to assume that no taxes were paid on the cash I handed him in return for his work. When he was done clearing our driveway, I made sure to get his telephone number, figuring I would call him the next time we had a major snowfall.

Sure enough, a few days later, an even bigger storm

hit. But when I called the fellow who had shoveled my driveway for $100, I got no answer. I left word for him to call me back, but he never did. I suspected it was because the continuing snow had created a high demand for his services.

Then, lo and behold, a kid came to our door and said his dad had a snow blower and would remove the snow from our driveway for $20. I couldn't believe it. Without government regulation to thwart him, here was a man who was undercutting the first snow-removal guy's price by 80 percent. Can anything be more beautiful than watching the free market in action? I could almost feel Henry Hazlitt smiling down on me. As with the first guy, I was sure to get his telephone number when he finished shoveling our driveway.

Enter snowstorm number three. After two days of non-stop snow, I called my $20 snow-shoveler, figuring that because of the depth of the snow, he might have decided to raise his price to $40 or $50. But I never found out, because all I got was his voicemail. I left word, but, again, no return call.

Staring at two feet of snow in my driveway, I was getting a bit concerned. Then, from out of nowhere, a lady came to my door and said that her husband had a snow-plow and asked if I would like him to remove the snow from our driveway for $65.

I wondered if I should take a pass on this offer and try again to connect with my $20 guy. But the thought occurred to me that he might be too busy to ever get back to me. Or what if he had discovered that his price was way under what the market would pay and had raised it to $75?

I pieced all of these factors together in my mind (a process that goes on billions of times a day in the marketplace), then added in the biggest factor of all—that the solution to my problem was standing right in front of me. No delay, no gamble, no stress—$65 it was.

The free-market aspect of my snow-shoveling experiences is obvious. But what I found even more interesting was that a handful of folks chose to engage in entrepreneurship by going out in the snow and cold, freezing their butts off, and working themselves to the point of exhaustion for a couple of thousand dollars a day, while 99.99 percent of those who say they can't find a job chose to sit at home and do . . . I guess whatever it is that unemployed people do when they sit at home.

If compassionate politicians are really serious about lowering unemployment, two good steps would be to eliminate unemployment benefits and abolish minimum-wage laws. Follow that with slashing the corporate tax rate to 10 percent (for starters), and unemployment would very quickly become an anachronism.

Capitalism is not a stationary or static system. It is a robust system, always changing, always evolving. The free market really does work—just not the way the Retrogressive would like it to work. The fact that so-called trickle-down economics not only works, but works especially well for those at the lower end of the economic ladder, drives him nuts and leaves him with no choice but to deride it as capitalist propaganda. The reality that unbridled capitalism is the best solution to poverty is a source of never-ending frustration for the Retrogressive.

Again, it's important to point out that it is the Entrepreneur's self-interest that is the driving force behind the success of capitalism. The invisible hand of the marketplace guarantees—repeat, *guarantees*—that, as a result of his quest for success, others will benefit from his efforts.

In fact, the Entrepreneur is almost always the *last* person in a venture to realize financial benefits. Employees and vendors, among others, must be paid if he is to stay in business, and he must stay in business in order to have any hope of eventually turning a profit for himself. As I said in Chapter 2, the Entrepreneur puts it all on the line every time out.

Too many high-profile capitalists try to defend capitalism by arguing that capitalists are motivated by altruism; i.e., that a capitalist's real desire is to help others, and, as a by-product, he, too, ends up benefiting financially. Whether such an argument is the result of ignorance or cowardice, it is patently untrue and misleading.

In truth, it's the other way around: In order to achieve his financial objectives, the smart Entrepreneur knows that he must create value for others. This is what drives competition. Thus, many people benefit as a result of the Entrepreneur's pursuit of his own financial objectives. Adam Smith referred to this phenomenon as the "unintended consequences" of capitalism.

Trying to claim that a true capitalist is altruistic insults the intelligence of the average worker. Of *course* the masses do not believe such nonsense, which is the kind of thing that makes them easy prey for socialist crusaders. While it is true that capitalism works best for the greatest number of people, that is not a moral justification for it. The moral justification for capitalism is that all men, no matter how rich or how poor, have a right to pursue their own economic well-being and enjoy all the fruits of their labor.

More specifically, all people have a right to trade their goods, their services, and their labor for any price they can secure in a free market, without interference from the government or anyone else. Freedom from all forms of coercion is a morally sound objective, *regardless* of whether the actions of free individuals benefit others. Fortunately, however, competition virtually guarantees that others *will* benefit.

Ownership

Absolute ownership is an essential element of freedom, and thus an essential element of capitalism and entrepreneurship. Yet, due to generations of Retrogressive brainwashing, it is a concept that many Americans seem unable to grasp. Those on the left continually preach (especially to schoolchildren) the moral importance of focusing on such abstracts as "the common good" and "social justice."

There is, of course, no such thing as the common good, because what is good for you may be bad for me, and vice versa. Civilized people work to improve their own well-being, and they do so while respecting the rights of others to do the same. But to the Retrogressive, the common good means basing your actions on *his* moral code. As to social justice, it is nothing more than a euphemism for redistribution of wealth, which can only be implemented by force.

The extent of an Entrepreneur's ability and motivation to create and produce is very much dependent on his feeling secure in the knowledge that when he creates something, it belongs to him—no strings attached. Common sense and morality dictate that he should not lose any of his ownership rights just because he is successful in building a highly profitable business. On the contrary, he should be admired, applauded, and emulated.

The Right to Establish the Rules

Ownership includes the Entrepreneur's right to operate his business his way. Take Walmart, which Sam Walton started with a single store in the tiny town of Rogers, Arkansas. Over time, he built the company into the largest employer in the United States, with more than 1.3 million employees. Thanks to the entrepreneurial genius and hard work of Sam Walton, Walmart saves consumers billions of dollars annually on their retail purchases.

Yet, for some years now, a growing number of disgruntled Walmart employees have been claiming that the company doesn't treat them "fairly."

As a consumer, of course, if you're sympathetic to their assertions, you have a remedy: You don't have to shop there! In economic circles, it's called "voting with your feet." Likewise, if you don't like the fact that Walmart carries too many products made in China or "sweatshop" countries, you can vote with your feet. Or if you're unhappy with Walmart because you believe it puts smaller retailers out of business by selling consumers what they want at lower prices . . . you guessed it, you can vote with your feet. In the words of the late Milton Friedman, you are free to choose.

But let's get back to Walmart's disgruntled employees. To the Retrogressive, their claims raise the question: What in the world can be done to protect the company's 1.3 million oppressed employees? (Never mind that Walmart employees earn, on average, about double the minimum wage.)

Even if we assume that there is such a thing as *absolute fairness*, and further assume that Walmart does, indeed, treat its employees unfairly, in a totally free society, unfair treatment of employees would never be an issue, because workers would be free to sell their services for the highest possible wages that they could secure in the open market. But if someone chooses to work at Walmart, that, by itself, is de facto proof that he believes, for any one of an infinite number of reasons, that it affords him the best opportunity to be adequately compensated for his skills, his experience, and his efforts.

An employer doesn't ask a job applicant to present a list of his job requirements when he submits his application.

On the contrary, the employer lets the applicant know, in advance, what the company's conditions of employment are. If those conditions include fifteen-hour workdays, minimum-wage pay, no paid sick leave, and no paid vacation time, so be it. Not only does a prospective employee not have to take such a job, an existing employee has a right to quit his job at any time.

And since the dissatisfied employee is free, he can apply for another job anywhere he chooses. No permission needed. On the other hand, if he decides to stay at his present place of employment, he is making a clear statement that he believes it's the best job he can hope to find at the wage he is being paid. If that were not so, he would have to be either insane or masochistic not to quit. Again, he is free to choose. Could anything be more fair than total freedom?

In a free marketplace, if a company's working conditions are too unfavorable, a competitor (probably many competitors) will offer better working conditions to lure the best employees away from that company. (I know, because I've done it myself many times over the years.) It's only when government bureaucrats or labor unions enter the picture that the freedom to bid openly for labor in the marketplace is violated. In a free market, everything works smoothly because both employers and employees are free to make their own choices.

All government intervention between employers and employees results in infringements on the rights of one or the other—or both. Freedom demands that consenting adults (including employers and employees, as well as business owners and consumers) be left alone to fend for themselves.

Thus, forcing a business owner to give "equal pay for equal work" is an act of aggression on the part of the government. The government simply has no constitutional authority to tell a business owner what he must pay his employees. Employees, after all, are not automatons. They are people, and every person has different skills, a different work ethic, and a different attitude. Speaking for myself, I place attitude at the top of the list, whereas government and unions place no value on it at all.

It's up to the business owner—and only the owner—to decide how much he wants to pay each of his employees, according to *his* judgment. What the government thinks is irrelevant, because the Constitution doesn't give it the authority to interfere with a privately owned business. A privately owned business is, by necessity, a dictatorship, but it's a unique dictatorship wherein the dictator cannot stop his employees from leaving whenever they wish.

The Right to Refuse Service

So does this mean that a restaurant has the right to refuse service to certain people? Yes! If a restaurant is really the property of an owner, that owner can make any rules he chooses for his business. And, contrary to popular belief, a privately owned business is *not* public property. It is *private* property.

In 2010, when MSNBC's Rachel Maddow asked Rand Paul (before his election to the U.S. Senate) if he believed that a private business should have the right to refuse service to African-Americans, he correctly answered, "Yes." He then went on to say, "I'm not in favor of discrimination of any form."

To many, Rand Paul's one-word answer and his follow-up comment might seem to contradict one another. The false assumption is that if someone believes a business owner has a right to refuse service to an African-American, that means he favors discrimination. The problem is that Maddow asked Paul what is commonly referred to as a *loaded question*. If you're going to be a serious supporter of liberty, you cannot allow yourself to be intimidated into answering loaded questions—i.e., questions based on a false premise or an implied false premise.

Here, the false premise was implied: If a business owner has the right to refuse service to someone, it automatically follows that that someone would be an African-American. But what if the owner of the business *is* an African-American? Like a white owner, a black owner has a right to do whatever he wishes with his business.

Again, the reason he possesses such a right is that it's *his* business. This simple fact is almost impossible for a Retrogressive to process, because he truly believes that he is intellectually and morally superior to the average person, from whence stems his belief that it is his duty to socially engineer the world to his liking.

What the Retrogressive cannot fathom is that skin

color is irrelevant to someone who believes in liberty. To believe that skin color is relevant to ability would be to undermine the very foundation upon which the true free-market Entrepreneur has built his life. By contrast, to the Retrogressive, the so-called race card is like oxygen. Without it, he and his antifreedom ideas would die. That's why, for decades, he has suffered withdrawal symptoms as race has become less and less of an issue in the United States.

As conservative economist Thomas Sowell has so often pointed out, if a business owner refuses to serve people purely on a discriminatory basis (such as race, ethnicity, or religion), he does so at his own peril, because the marketplace will punish him. (Speaking for myself, I would never patronize a company or restaurant that refused to serve people of *any* specific race or ethnicity, and I think I can safely say that I'm in the majority on that.) By the same token, if an employer wants to shortchange himself by limiting the advancement of certain kinds of people, the profit-oriented Entrepreneur will be more than happy to hire all the good talent that he does not want.

Legislating morals *does not work*. What is there about this self-evident truth that the Retrogressive does not understand?

Ownership is not a race issue; it's a liberty issue. Libertarian-centered conservatism and racism are mutually exclusive beliefs. The real problem is that Retrogressive government's refusal to acknowledge private ownership rights is a major impediment to entrepreneurship.

Labor Unions

Unions are the antithesis of free enterprise and are a never-ending drag on, and threat to, a nation's economy. The actions of most labor unions are in violation of Natural Law and the constitutional rights of both employees and employers.

The so-called union shop violates the rights of every employee who is forced to join a union against his will. Worse, it violates the right of an employer to hire whomever he wants, whenever he wants, for whatever reasons are important to *him*.

Thanks to labor unions, we've had decades of artificially high wages and benefits, job-protection schemes, and government-mandated safety standards—with spoiled American workers demanding still more, even while watching their jobs being exported to other countries. What good is a union wage if there are no jobs? Still, unions can usually count on government support, which became almost embarrassingly evident after Retrogressives took control of the House, the Senate, and the executive branch of the federal government in 2009.

A good example of this support is when the National Mediation Board came up with a proposal to make it easier for airline and railroad workers to unionize. For seventy-five years, the rule had been that in order for any class of workers (e.g., pilots) employed by an airline or railroad to unionize, a majority of all employees in that class had to vote for unionization. By contrast, the proposed new rule requires only that a majority of employees who actually vote on the question of unionization is needed to unionize.

The real question should be whether employees should be allowed to unionize *at all* without the consent of their employer.

The proposed National Right to Work Act would give workers the right to work in a "union shop" without joining the union, which is certainly a step in the right direction, but it still fails to acknowledge the owner's right to dictate the terms of employment for his own business. Not only do I believe that workers do not have a right to unionize a company through tyranny of the majority, I don't believe that *any* worker has a right to join a union without the consent of his employer. If ownership is to have any real meaning, then an owner can set whatever rules he chooses for his business. If he can't do that, he cannot be considered an owner in the true sense of the word.

I should point out here that size is irrelevant when it comes to a business owner's right to operate his business the way he chooses. If a business grows large and has millions of shareholders, it is the property of those shareholders. Thus, the only relevance size has is that when property rights are violated against a large corporation as opposed to a single-owner proprietorship, it simply means that far more people are victims of government aggression. It is a moral absurdity to believe that bigness validates aggression.

Having said this, regardless of the size of a business, the *only* way unionization is morally valid is if the owner of that business voluntarily agrees to it. It's *his* business. It's *his* property. And it is *his* human right to set the rules for his own property. For the Entrepreneur to devote his full time and attention to creating profits, he must feel secure in the knowledge that his property rights will always be protected. Such protection is one of the key *legitimate* functions of government.

It can't be repeated too often: In a truly free society, a worker has one inalienable, overpowering right with regard to his job—he can quit at any time. He is not a slave, so his employer cannot chain him to his work. If he wants to belong to a union, he is free to search for employment with a company that allows workers to unionize.

This is precisely the kind of issue that has caused conservative politicians to lose their way over the years. Until they have the courage to confront unionization head on and stop buying into debates about how much or how little an owner's property rights should be violated, unions will continue to be a major obstacle for the Entrepreneur and thus a major obstacle to job creation, a healthy economy, and a better standard of living for everyone.

The Indians Are Coming!

What's this world coming to? The Mexicans have been attacking us from the south, and now the Indians are attacking us from . . . well, from halfway around the world—in their own country! Let me explain.

If we want Mexicans to pick our grapes and mow our lawns—and the fact is that we do—they have to come to the United States to do so. But to get the brainy work done at bargain rates doesn't require any sandals on the ground in the United States. Instead, we can send our accounting, MRI scanning business, and customer-service needs to India.

Indians—hardworking, quality-conscious, action-oriented, ambitious, creative Indians—are on the brink of out-entrepreneuring us. *Time* magazine, in its June 26, 2006, cover story titled "India Inc.," opined that the ingenuity of India's people is *the* indispensable asset that has sustained its democracy and catapulted it to being on the verge of becoming a global power.

Best of all, India might just save America from itself—or at least postpone its day of reckoning. By insourcing so many important tasks at one-third to one-fifth the labor cost in America, it is saving U.S. companies billions of dollars. That money, in turn, allows those companies to invest in producing products that Americans can still manufacture better than anyone else—which, in turn, increases employment and circulates more wealth throughout our economy.

And with China turning out all the ticky-tacky stuff we've convinced ourselves we need—such essentials as back scrubbers, clock radios, belt racks, and toasters—at bargain-basement prices, Americans can still afford to blow a few hundred bucks on a pair of tickets to a pro football or basketball game, eat out a few nights a week, and enjoy a couple of fun-and-sun vacations each year. Which means that everyone wins: Indians get wealthier by the day and Americans are able to continue deluding themselves into believing that they're still wealthy.

The *Time* article ended on a couple of sobering notes that few Americans are ready to accept. The first was a quotation from Thomas Friedman's *The World Is Flat*: "The jobs will go to those who can do them best, in the most cost-effective manner. Geography is irrelevant." Even a liberal like Thomas Friedman gets it, but labor-union leaders refuse to accept the realities of the marketplace.

Unions can demand any wages they want, but so long as there are people in "sweatshops" all over the world who are willing to do the same jobs at a fraction of those wages, it proves that union pay is artificially high and out of line with the supply and demand of the marketplace.

The second sobering note from that *Time* article is a quotation from Marc Faber, a highly respected emerging-markets investor based in Hong Kong and Thailand: "If someone put a gun to my head and said, 'You have to put all your money in India or all of it in the U.S.,' I'd choose India."[4]

The Retrogressive loves to rail about the injustice of "sweatshops" in India and other developing countries. But isn't it amazing how those nasty little sweatshops have a way of improving the lives of the very people who produce the sweat, notwithstanding the protestations of the Retrogressive, who still longs for a utopian world where all workers toil in an atmosphere of total comfort? The reality is that so-called sweatshops (euphemism for *employment opportunities come true*) in such places as India, Indonesia, and Pakistan have been a godsend to millions of previously desperate, unemployed people.

In his book *Myths, Lies, and Downright Stupidity,* John Stossel relates a conversation he had with an Indian economist, Bibek Debroy. When Stossel asked him about the issue of sweatshops that seems to have so many Retrogressives in America upset, Debroy responded, "I don't understand the expression 'sweatshops.' There's nothing wrong with sweat. Sweat is good! Sweat is what most people in the developing world, including India, do all the time."

Stossel goes on to say that sweat not only puts food on the table, it puts a roof *over* the table. The clothing factories that protesters call sweatshops are exactly the same kind of businesses that helped people in now thriving places like South Korea, Taiwan, and Hong Kong escape poverty.[5]

A few years back, I did some business with a company in Bangalore, India. After we got to know each other a bit, the CEO of the company said to me, "Robert, I'm going to tell you something that you'll thank me for someday. Come to Bangalore for a few weeks, and I guarantee that you'll leave with a hundred new ideas for making money. Bangalore is the entrepreneurial capital of the world."

Since India is also the snake capital of the world (or perhaps tied with Australia for that honor), I didn't go. But I believed him. India, China, and other developing countries are focused on growth, so they have developed great respect for entrepreneurship. They also have very little tolerance for those who harbor an anticapitalist mentality.

Capitalism's Eternal Nemesis: Regulation

The new Asian economic powerhouses are well aware that if regulation is anything, it is antigrowth. In that respect, they're laughing all the way to the boardroom as American Retrogressives press for ever more entrepreneurism-stifling regulation in the United States.

Regulation—local, state, and, especially, federal—is perhaps the Entrepreneur's main nemesis. But to the Retrogressive, it is the answer to most of the world's perceived ills. Thus, the Entrepreneur is faced with a never-ending stream of regulations, or threatened regulations, such as government-controlled healthcare, environmental controls (especially "cap and trade"), financial regulatory reform, the Food Safety and Modernization Act, and bans on oil drilling, coal mining, and the building of nuclear power plants.

Generally speaking, regulations have the effect of preventing people from doing things they *want* to do or forcing them to do things they *don't* want to do. Either way, regulations suppress entrepreneurship and creativity, which in turn slows the economy and makes people less well off. Worse, government regulations give people a false sense of security, because they erroneously believe that the government possesses an inherently superior ability to know what is best for them.

When Congressman Darrell Issa, chairman of the House Committee on Oversight and Government Reform, sent letters to companies asking which regulations they found particularly burdensome, the committee's ranking member, Democrat Elijah Cummings of Maryland, said in an interview with MSNBC, "If you look at big business and you ask them what is it they don't like about regulation, they're going to probably send you a list of things that will allow them to make more money."[6]

Golly, what a terrible thought. We wouldn't want companies to make too much money. After all, that might cause them to expand their businesses, create more jobs, and stimulate the economy (and, yes, pay more taxes). The idea of free enterprise (companies regulating themselves through the natural market forces of supply and demand) is so foreign to politicians like Cummings that they assume everyone agrees it would be a bad thing to cut back on regulations.

Following is a small sampling of regulations that hamstring the Entrepreneur and, as a result, do endless harm to the economy and the well-being of all Americans.

The Minimum Wage

There will always be those who want to remove wages from free-market constraints, but as a job-killer, the minimum wage is right up there with unemployment benefits. Plus, it's another example of government's refusal to respect ownership rights and to refrain from intervening in a matter that is not permitted by the Constitution.

No one—especially a politician or government bureaucrat—has a right to force an employer to pay any specific wage. A business is an extension of the owner's life, and no one has a right to interfere with another individual's life. Likewise, a prospective employee has a natural right to sell his services in the marketplace for any wage that is acceptable to him.

In mandating a so-called minimum wage, government creates unemployment by preventing transactions between consenting adults (employers and employees) who have every right to agree on a wage that is acceptable to both of them.

Just to annoy any Retrogressive who may be reading this book, I'll say it one more time before moving on: A prospective employee cannot be forced to take a job with any company whose pay or working conditions are not satisfactory to him. And a current employee who is dissatisfied with his employer's pay or working conditions is free to quit his job at any time. He doesn't even have to give a reason—or notice!

Thus, the minimum wage is a curse not only to the Entrepreneur, but to prospective employees and the overall economy. In a true laissez-faire economy, anyone who wanted to work would have a job. The only way an individual could be unemployed would be if he preferred starvation to taking a job at a wage that was determined by supply and demand.

Universal Healthcare

The Retrogressive loves regulation, because, in his mind, it's a way of making the world a better place by forcing the intellectually inferior masses to abide by guidelines that he believes bring about "social justice." He also knows that once regulations are passed, they not only are very difficult to repeal, but also have a tendency to expand rather than contract.

That's why many Retrogressive activists who view government-run healthcare as the crown jewel of a redistribution-of-wealth society have explained to their followers that the game plan is to "get our foot in the door" with some form of government-regulated healthcare. Then, once that is accomplished, it would only be a matter of time before the federal government would take over the entire healthcare system.

Numerous audios, videos, and written statements to this effect are available online. Thus, it was no mystery why Barack Obama and his Retrogressive allies in Congress pushed through Obamacare on Christmas Eve 2009, realizing that the Tea Party movement was poised to overwhelm them at the polls the following November.

The idea that "we all agree that some kind of healthcare reform is needed" is akin to Al Gore's saying that "the debate on global warming is over." The only reform that is needed is for the government to get 100 percent *out* of the healthcare business—*including* Medicare and Medicaid—and let insurance companies vie for customers in a free-market environment. A truly free market is *always* fair, because people are free to buy the product *they* want—whether it be healthcare or any other commodity.

Even if the current healthcare monstrosity is overturned by the Supreme Court or ultimately gets repealed, I fear that, sooner or later, some form of government-related healthcare bill will be passed, regardless of what a majority of American serfs want. And if that occurs, the one thing of which we can be certain is that small businesses will be the hardest hit—not only with higher taxes, but by a huge increase in paperwork.

Of course, Barack Obama's buddies can get waivers to opt out of his healthcare program, but such waivers are not available to the Entrepreneur. On the contrary, he is left to pay the lion's share of the bill for those who receive special treatment.

As we have already seen, healthcare legislation that involves the government in any way increases operating costs for small businesses across the board. And all-out government-run healthcare could bring the Entrepreneur to his creative knees and be the death knell of the American economy if it were ever fully implemented. The higher cost of doing business would cause small firms to lay off employees, which would increase unemployment, increase jobless benefits, and, again, further depress the economy.

Worse, many small businesses would simply shut their doors, either voluntarily or through involuntary liquidation. Any way you slice it, the biggest cost of government-run healthcare to all of us would be its devastating effect on the engine of our economy—the Entrepreneurs who operate 27 million small businesses and create 75 percent of all new jobs. Given the skyrocketing costs that have resulted from Medicare and Medicaid, that should be evident to virtually anyone who pays even the slightest attention to the economy.

Environmental Regulations

Rachel Carson, the legendary environmentalist who wrote the tree-hugger classic *Silent Spring* (1962), is a perfect example of a Retrogressive whose ideas had disastrous unintended consequences on the lives of millions of people. Her book led to a ban on the pesticide DDT, and many authorities believe that this ban still causes more than a million malarial deaths a year in Africa.

Retrogressives have gotten so wacky that now they've invented something called "environmental rights." Talk about abstract concepts. Create the crisis of your choice— global warming, education, oil-price gouging, home foreclosures—then milk the fabricated crisis nonstop until Americans are convinced that the only solution to the crisis is for government to step in and pass more laws and create more regulations to save us from imminent peril.

Sadly, every one of those new laws and regulations makes it more difficult for the Entrepreneur to put his creativity to work to produce products and services that can improve people's lives. This puts the American Entrepreneur at a tremendous disadvantage when it comes to competing with Entrepreneurs in countries such as China, India, and Taiwan, where the government does not burden them with endless regulations.

Nevertheless, Retrogressive organizations such as Defenders of Wildlife, Earthjustice, Environment America, World Wildlife Fund, Friends of the Earth, and the Environmental Defense Fund press relentlessly forward, still dreaming of a return to a time when people traveled by horse and buggy, ate only farm-fresh foods, were much healthier than they are today, and were happy with less—indeed, a time that never existed!

Manure-filled dirt streets, crop failures, and widespread disease were closer to the reality of those preindustrialized days when the average American could expect to live about fifty years. But the Retrogressive has no interest in reality, and his stubborn refusal to acknowledge the facts translates into a never-ending stream of regulations that impede the progress of the Entrepreneur and his ability to move civilization forward.

An *a priori* argument is one in which a person's conclusion is masked as a premise, and one of the best examples of this is global warming. Though their theories have been repeatedly discredited, the Gorist crowd refuses to give up. They still insist that "the causal link between man-made emissions and global warming has been firmly established." (Side note: As I write this, more than half the nation is being pummeled by freezing temperatures, snow, and ice, and probably wishing that global warming would hurry up and arrive.)

In this regard, I recall another cover story in *Time*—this one on global warming (*before* our recent Ice Age winters descended upon us and made frostbite a bigger concern to the average person than heat stroke)—that inundated readers with *a priori* arguments. The title of the article on the magazine's cover was a teaser to warm you up (pun intended): "BE WORRIED. BE **VERY** WORRIED."

Following that were these words: "Climate change isn't some vague future problem—it's already damaging the planet at an alarming pace. Here's how it affects you, your kids and their kids as well."

I don't have the inclination or space to print every *a priori* argument in the magazine's fourteen-page article, but here's one that's too good to pass up: "Global warming, even most skeptics have concluded, is the real deal, and human activity has been causing it."[7]

To appreciate the absurdity of this statement, type in "global warming skeptics" on Google. I did, and I found 726,000 listings. I guess the thousands of scientists and investigative journalists who have studied this phenomenon and arrived at a different conclusion don't count. Here's an example from one of my favorite writers, British journalist/author Melanie Phillips:

Wrong, wrong, wrong, and wrong. There is no such evidence. The whole thing is a global scam. There is no firm evidence that warming is happening; [and] even if it is, it is most likely to have natural, not man-made, causes. Carbon dioxide, supposedly the culprit, makes up such a tiny fraction of the atmosphere that even if it were to quadruple, the effect on climate would be negligible. And just about every one of the eco-doomster stories that curdle our blood every five minutes is either speculative, ahistorical or scientifically illiterate.[8]

I am not for or against the idea of global warming. It may be happening, or maybe not. But I can't help but recall the dire warnings in the 1970s and early 1980s from scientists, politicians, and special-interest groups about the dangers we were facing from global *cooling*—that we simply could not afford to gamble, that we couldn't risk inaction, and that those scientists who disagreed on the issue of global cooling were acting irresponsibly. And many of the scientists who are now sounding the alarm about global warming are the very same ones who were warning everyone about global cooling twenty years ago!

The *a priori* argument is usually employed by people who have an agenda. The end result is an excuse for government to ride in on its white horse and save the day by passing more legislation—legislation that puts the American Entrepreneur at a tremendous disadvantage when it comes to competing with Entrepreneurs in countries such as China, India, and Taiwan, where government does not plague them with endless regulations.

Energy Regulations

Energy regulations go hand in hand with environmental regulations, because environmentalist freaks are the biggest obstacle to making America energy independent and keeping the price of our gas and oil down. I've always felt that a visitor from another galaxy would conclude that America's energy policy—if one wants to make the argument that it even has an energy policy—has been planned and carried out by emotionally disturbed individuals, ignoramuses, or those who are intent on ending America's dominance as the world's only superpower. (My bet would be on the last, beginning with Barack Obama.)

The crown jewel of the Obamaviks' artificial energy-crisis strategy is the skyrocketing price of gasoline, resulting almost exclusively from government's heavy-handed, unconstitutional regulation of the petroleum industry.

If you think the cost of filling up your tank has been a financial burden, just imagine how it's interfered with the Entrepreneur's ability to build a business. Consider the Entrepreneur who is dependent on a gas-guzzling truck to get his goods to his customers. If the price of gas had been anywhere near where it is today, I couldn't have even considered expanding the little produce business that got my entrepreneurial career going. And that's not to mention the damper that increased regulations put on an Entrepreneur's ability to come up with creative ways to service the petroleum industry itself.

As an example of these regulations, in early 2011 the Environmental Protection Agency (EPA) handed down a ruling to withhold "air permits" from Shell Oil, which, in essence, forced the company to drop its long-planned exploration project in the Arctic Ocean off the northern coast of Alaska. The result was that Shell wasted five years and roughly $4 billion in preparation for the project. The EPA's excuse for its "drill nowhere, drill never" ruling was that Shell's exploration would have been too close (seventy miles) to a one-square-mile village named Kaktovik, a booming metropolis of 245 residents!

Needless to say, far-left groups like the Center for Biological Diversity and the Alaska Wilderness League were wetting their pants with joy at their victory. No big deal—just another 27 billion barrels of oil that have been left to sit underground indefinitely. When the news reached Riyadh, they must have been passing out celebratory cookies in the streets.

Retrogressives love to rail about greedy oil companies making billions of dollars in profits, but most everyone who watches or reads the news knows that the profit margins in the oil industry are relatively small compared to, say, those of technology companies like Facebook, Google, and Microsoft. All other things being equal, the chief cause of rising oil prices is the continuing decline of the dollar.

Which ties the artificial oil crisis to the equally artificial debt-ceiling crisis, because when you raise the debt ceiling, as Congress has been doing nonstop for decades, it makes it possible for the government to spend more, which in turn causes the dollar to decline.

Everyone is familiar with the famous line from George Orwell's *Animal Farm,* "All animals are equal, but some animals are more equal than others." I think about this line whenever I hear a debate about drilling for oil in Alaska's Arctic National Wildlife Refuge (ANWR). For decades, the save-the-world-from-humans crowd has blocked oil drilling in ANWR by arguing, at least in part, that it would be harmful to the caribou that hang out there.

So as to keep this simple, let's forget, for the moment, that there is no evidence whatsoever that caribou would in any way be harmed by oil drilling. Let's also ignore the fact that caribou do not seem to be the least bit fazed when oil workers are bustling about nearby. Let's even disbelieve reports from firsthand observers who say that caribou often sidle up to the Alaskan pipeline because they appear to like the warmth.

Yep, let's forget all of the above and stipulate, just for the fun of it, that oil drilling somehow puts caribou "in harm's way." But even if that were the case, the truth is that some people—gasp!—don't give a damn about the caribou. We all know how "downright mean" Americans are.

Of course, everything I've said here is moot anyway, because the truth is that oil drilling anywhere in Alaska would not harm one hair on the head of any caribou.

Retrogressives need to stop playing God by unilaterally deciding which animals should be protected and which are okay to slaughter by the billions, year in and year out. In their arrogant, self-righteous vision of the world, some animals really are more equal than others. Given that the Retrogressive extols the virtues of eugenics, I guess that shouldn't surprise anyone.

Now that nuclear reactors have people a bit skittish—especially considering that the powers that be brilliantly built so many of them on or near earthquake faults—it's all the more reason that we should be drilling everywhere possible. And, in addition, clean coal mining, as well as oil-shale mining, should be set free to help eliminate America's dependence on foreign energy sources.

The United States has at least one hundred years of natural gas reserves and two hundred years of coal reserves. And I'd wager that if all restrictions were lifted, we'd discover that we have much greater oil reserves than is now believed. The artificial oil crisis could be solved overnight by:

1. Closing down the Department of Energy and the EPA, and getting the government *completely* out of the energy business.

2. Making oil and gas drilling legal everywhere—in the Gulf, off both coasts, even in your backyard—no restrictions and no exceptions.

3. Cutting taxes to *zero* on all oil companies, both large and small.

4. Removing *all* taxes on gas at the pump for consumers.

All this would result in hundreds of billions of dollars in increased profits for oil companies, which, in turn, would result in:

1. The creation of hundreds of thousands of new jobs (and millions more indirectly), which would actually *increase* tax revenues for those greedy guys who roam the halls of Congress.

2. Oil companies increasing, rather than decreasing, exploration and production, which would put the United States on a fast track to becoming energy independent and increase the opportunities for Entrepreneurs interested in pursuing industry-related ventures.

3. Oil companies paying higher dividends to their shareholders, most of whom are mutual funds and pension funds, which would translate into more money for middle-class Americans to spend.

To reiterate what I said earlier, regulation—local, state, and, especially, federal—is perhaps the Entrepreneur's main nemesis. In a marketplace devoid of most government regulations, the economy and job creation would explode, and virtually everyone would enjoy a better and more prosperous life.

Try as he may to transform the world into a collectivist paradise, the Retrogressive is constantly faced with the truth: Capitalism/free enterprise is the foundation for entrepreneurship, and entrepreneurship leads to creativity, wealth creation, a booming economy, and jobs for everyone who wants to work.

5.

The Anti-entrepreneurial

Holy Grail

Let there be no doubt in anyone's mind: The anti-entrepreneurial Holy Grail of Retrogressivism is redistribution of wealth. In raw terms, what this amounts to is taking money from some individuals (Entrepreneurs and other productive members of society) and handing it to others. Of course, the actual transfer is done in myriad ways that obfuscate the fact that wealth is changing hands through the threat of force.

The most obvious method for transferring wealth is to raise taxes on the (perceived) rich, which is really just a euphemism for raising taxes on the middle class. The reason taxes on the rich always end up being taxes on the middle class is that there aren't enough rich people to make a dent in the transfer-of-wealth schemes of Retrogressive politicians. But as even the most ardent socialist knows, there's a limit to how much you can raise taxes. Because when tax rates increase, those at whom the taxes are aimed become less motivated to produce, thus the amount of taxes collected actually decreases.

The politician's second alternative when it comes to raising money for his redistribution-of-wealth programs is to borrow it. This method lowers the standard of living of producers while funding programs that provide other people with either money or services at little or no cost to them. However, with our debt now nearing $16 trillion (at the time of the writing of this book), the days of being able to borrow limitless sums of money will soon be behind us. It's only a matter of time until China and other countries cut us off or raise interest rates so high that the government will not have enough revenue to pay anything other than interest on the national debt.

The most subtle and effective means of redistributing wealth is through currency inflation, which in turn leads to price inflation. Printing paper dollars (or simply making digital entries in government computers) is the "solution" most preferred by politicians, because it allows them to have their cake and eat it, too. That's because, as most everyone serious enough to be reading this book knows, inflation is a hidden tax. By printing up enough "money" to cover the remainder of each year's deficit, politicians get off the hook because they don't have to vote for tax increases.

However, recklessly increasing the money supply leads to hyperinflation, and once hyperinflation hits the United States, most people will have no understanding of the cause. As a result, they will be all too willing to take up the government's battle cry to "fight inflation." And how do you fight inflation? By pointing a finger at all the wrong parties, of course. When politicians accuse big business and "greedy" capitalists of causing inflation, they know they are lying.

The danger with hyperinflation is that it can quickly lead to a runaway-inflation scenario. And when that happens, commercial transactions become almost impossible to engage in, because people are not willing to accept paper money in exchange for their goods and services. And because very few people understand what is causing prices to rise out of control, the move toward a dictatorship begins to look appealing to them. (The Weimar Republic's runaway inflation in 1923, followed by Adolf Hitler's rise to power, is a charming little example of this.)

False Premises

The problem with most political debates is that they are based on false premises. The key to most of these false premises is that they ignore both Natural Law and the Constitution. The classic example of this is redistribution of wealth, which takes resources from the Entrepreneur and other productive citizens and gives it to nonproducers.

On a broad scale, virtually all congressional debates over how much money should be appropriated to this or that social program are based on the false premise that the government possesses the right to do things that are not spelled out in the Constitution—such as spending your money without your consent.

The question of constitutional authority should always be established before entering into a discussion of the pros and cons of any government program, no matter how well intended any such program may be. In the vast majority of cases, the answer to this question would eliminate the need for further debate.

Following are some other examples of false premises used to justify the Retrogressive's redistribution-of-wealth policies.

It is the government's duty to provide for the "general welfare."

Elected officials and Supreme Court justices have made redistribution of wealth their main function by "elasticizing" their interpretation of the Constitution. First and foremost, they would have us believe that the term *general welfare* in the Constitution implies that the government has the power to fulfill the needs and desires of individual citizens.

In particular, they point to Article 1, Section 8, Clause 1 of the Constitution, which states, in part: "The Congress shall have power to lay and collect taxes, duties, imposts and excises, to pay the debts and provide for the common defence and general welfare of the United States."

The argument is preposterous on its face, because the term "general welfare of the United States" immediately follows "provide for the common defence." Together, "provide for the common defence *and* general welfare of the United States" makes it clear that the drafters of the Constitution were referring to the general welfare of the country, not the welfare of specific individuals.

The preamble to the Constitution alludes to promoting (as opposed to providing for) "the general welfare," but, similarly, it follows the words "provide for the common defence." Again, to attempt to stretch the term "general welfare" to imply the welfare of individuals is absurd.

When Barack Obama began violating the Constitution the day he took office, it wasn't because he was not aware of what the Constitution said. That was made clear in a 2001 radio interview, when he stated:

> *The Supreme Court never ventured into the issues of redistribution of wealth, and of more basic issues such as political and economic justice in society. To that extent, as radical as I think people try to characterize the Warren Court, it wasn't that radical. It didn't break free from the essential constraints that were placed by the Founding Fathers in the Constitution, at least as it's been interpreted and the Warren Court interpreted in the same way, that generally the Constitution is a charter of negative liberties.[1]*

Why hasn't the Supreme Court ever ventured into the matter of redistribution of wealth? And what in the world were the Founding Fathers thinking about when they failed to broach the subject? Surely, it must have been an oversight that they never addressed the issue of taking your assets and giving them to your neighbor. Or perhaps it's just an indication that George Washington, Benjamin Franklin, and James Madison were cold, callous individuals who enjoyed watching people suffer.

In the same radio interview, Obama went on to say that the Constitution:

[says] what the federal government can't do to you, but doesn't say what the federal government or state government must do on your behalf, and that hasn't shifted . . . and one of the, I think, tragedies of the civil rights movement was . . . um . . . because the civil rights movement became so court focused I think there was a tendency to lose track of the political and community organizing and activities on the ground that are able to put together the actual coalition of powers through which you bring about redistributive change.²

Excuse me? Do on *your* behalf? Those stupid Founding Fathers again. They didn't even think to put in the Constitution what the government must do on your behalf (code for what it can do *to* you). What in the world were those mentally challenged old white guys thinking?

And what a tragedy it was that the civil rights movement didn't put together the coalition of powers that could bring about "redistributive change." Forget the fact that the Constitution never mentions the redistribution of *anything*. We all know that redistribution of wealth is the only moral way for a civilized country to function, right?

All this makes it easier to understand one of Obama's early slips from behind his stealth moderate veil when he made his famous comment to Joe the Plumber, "I think when you spread the wealth around, it's good for everybody." Usurpers of the Constitution like Barack Obama would do well to remember two of Ron Paul's "Six Forgotten Principles of Freedom":

1. The justification for the existence of government is to protect the liberty of individuals, not to redistribute wealth or pass out special privileges.

2. People's lives and actions are their own responsibility, not the government's.[3]

The fact that the Entrepreneur continues to move mankind forward in spite of the widely accepted belief that redistribution of wealth is a morally justified activity of government is remarkable on its face. But to the Retrogressive, neither facts nor morals are important. The Retrogressive always remains laser focused on the belief that entrepreneurship and capitalism are evil and must be destroyed.

If all redistribution-of-wealth policies were suddenly to be eliminated, the Entrepreneur would be free to create a world of plenty—and that would be devastating to the Retrogressive.

People who earn a lot of money do so by "exploiting" the poor.

The words *exploiting the poor* are code for paying people wages they are willing to accept and selling them products and services at prices that are agreeable to them—all without coercion. "Exploiting the poor" is just another in a long list of abstract Retrogressive catchphrases that have no real meaning.

Unfortunately, the premise that successful Entrepreneurs got where they are by exploiting the poor promotes another false premise: that if you have "made it" financially, you have a moral obligation to hand over an ever larger share of your earnings to the government to redistribute to those less fortunate than you. Both of these false premises go virtually unchallenged by even the most conservative members of Congress and the media.

The endless parade of Retrogressives on television continues to spew out juvenile, soak-the-rich, class-warfare rhetoric that not only ignores the facts (e.g., that the top 1 percent of earners already pay more than 40 percent of all income taxes) but conveniently ignores moral considerations as well. They unfailingly base their arguments on the premise that taking from those who have managed to work their way into the top income bracket is morally justified.

That being the case, they have no feelings for the (perceived) rich person. In plotting their do-gooder schemes, it's quite easy for them to ignore a successful

Entrepreneur's right to his life and liberty. They see nothing wrong with encroaching on his freedom for the "public good." Bring out the guillotine! From whence comes another in a long line of brilliant Joe Biden statements: "We don't call it redistribution. We call it fairness."

What the Retrogressive politician is essentially saying to the Entrepreneur is: "America is the land of opportunity, and we're pulling for your success. But if you succeed 'too much,' we will take an increasingly larger percentage of your earnings and redistribute it to those *we* deem to be in need. So please keep working hard, because your success will provide more money for us to redistribute to others." What a terrific way to incentivize people.

Compassion justifies aggression.

People have a natural right to be free to make personal choices about their own lives, their own bodies, and their own property. That's what Natural Law is all about.

If one believes it is a violation of an individual's natural right to force him to do something he does not want to do (e.g., give up part of his wealth or property to others) or prevent him from doing something that he does want to do (so long as his actions do not harm anyone else), then government aggression can never be morally justified. In a society of moral people, the Law of Nonaggression (Natural Law) would be the only law that would be necessary.

Where confusion sets in is in the Retrogressive's perversion of a uniquely human trait known as *compassion*.

Contrary to what some animal lovers would like to believe, animals, in the strictest sense of the word, do not have the capacity to be compassionate. Only human beings can feel compassion, and they can feel it for both people and animals.

Which, of course, is a good thing. It's why private charity thrives in America, notwithstanding the fact that the government forces individuals to hand over a substantial portion of their earnings to fund immoral and unconstitutional government activities. Compassion is about charity, and charity is about each individual giving not according to his ability, but according to his *desire*—to those whom *he* deems to be in need and worthy of his charity.

The Retrogressive, however, does not see it that way. He chooses to sever the relationship between compassion and charity and instead links compassion with aggression—i.e., the use of force. And while it may seem self-evident that compassion and aggression contradict one another, thanks to the emotion of guilt, this combination is an easy sell even to those who possess a basic belief in individual sovereignty.

After all, how can a person not be in favor of taking wealth from "rich" people when millions are unemployed . . . homeless . . . in need of medical treatment . . . lacking money for education . . . the list is endless, because human desires/needs are endless. But a person would have to be omniscient, not to mention divinely moral, to know which needs of which people are superior to the rights of other individuals to keep what is theirs.

Since the government does not create wealth, the only way it can "help" people—whether to give them unemployment benefits, healthcare, or any other commodity—is to commit aggression against others and use force to take the resources it needs. This does not present a moral problem for the Retrogressive, because he is convinced that the means necessary to redistribute wealth and power according to his wishes are always justifiable.

In Amity Shlaes's book *The Forgotten Man,* she quotes Yale philosopher William Graham Sumner, who, in an 1883 essay, explained the crux of the moral problem with retrogressivism as follows: "As soon as A observes something which seems to him to be wrong, from which X is suffering, A talks it over with B, and A and B then propose to get a law passed to remedy the evil and help X. Their law always proposes to determine . . . what A, B, and C shall do for X."

Shlaes then goes on to add: "But what about C? There was nothing wrong with A and B helping X. What was wrong was the law, and the indenturing of C to the cause. C was the forgotten man, the man who paid, 'the man who never is thought of.'" [4]

In other words, C is the guy who isn't bothering anyone, but who is *forced* to supply the funds to help the X's of the world, those whom power holders unilaterally decide have been treated unfairly and must be compensated in order to achieve "social justice."

FDR, however, did a switcheroo on Sumner's point by removing the moniker of "the forgotten man" from C and giving it to X—"the poor man, the old man, laborer, or any other recipient of government help." FDR originally used the phrase *the forgotten man* to refer to the victims of the Dust Bowl in the 1930s. Zap! Just like that, Sumner's forgotten man was transformed into the opposite of what he was meant to be.

In truth, it is the Entrepreneur who is the epitome of the forgotten man. His desire to get ahead in life by creating and building products valued in the marketplace, and, in the process, making money and creating jobs and a better life for others, is never given a second thought by the Retrogressive. That's why the Entrepreneur is always the one who is hardest hit by the lethal combination of higher taxes and more regulations.

In his essay, Sumner went on to say:

All history is only one long story to this effect: men have struggled for power over their fellow-men in order that they might win the joys of earth at the expense of others and might shift the burdens of life from their own shoulders upon those of others. It is true that, until this time, the proletariat, the mass of mankind, have rarely had the power and they have not made such a record as kings and nobles and priests have made of the abuses they would perpetrate against their fellow-men when they could and dared.

But what folly it is to think that vice and passion are limited by classes, that liberty consists only in

*taking power away from nobles and priests and giv-
ing it to artisans and peasants and that these latter
will never abuse it! They will abuse it just as all others have done unless they are put under checks and
guarantees, and there can be no civil liberty anywhere
unless rights are guaranteed against all abuses, as well
from proletarians as from generals, aristocrats, and
ecclesiastics.*[5]

Sumner was a man of great insight. He recognized that history has demonstrated that the premise that the poor are morally superior to the rich is baseless. This is where I believe sincere revolutionaries go wrong. While their initial intentions (to help "the poor") may, at least in their own minds, be well-intentioned, they begin with a false premise (that the misfortunes of those at the bottom of the economic ladder are a result of being "exploited" by those who are more successful) and, from there, leap from one false conclusion to another.

Only a Retrogressive would even attempt to rationalize why the use of force is morally superior to charity. The idea that compassion justifies aggression is a perversity that must be exposed for what it is: an excuse for government to increase its power over people. On the other hand, as such Entrepreneurs as Bill Gates have proven, compassion leads quite naturally to charity, without government involvement. Pretty simple, I would say—and self-evident.

The growing gap between the rich and the poor is immoral and proves that capitalism has failed.

I have never heard anyone—neither politicians, nor media pundits, nor their guests—challenge the premise that "the growing gap between the rich and the poor" is a bad thing. Not once. Yet, the politically incorrect truth is that the gap between the rich and the poor is *supposed* to increase under capitalism. It's built into the system. But also built into the system is the fact that almost *everyone* is better off under capitalism.

Let us, for the moment, ignore the question of who has the omniscience and moral authority to decide who is rich and who is poor. In a mythical, totally free society, if everyone were to start with nothing, it is inarguable that some people would become more well off than others. Now, stop and think about that for a moment. Wouldn't natural market forces assure that the most successful people would become even more successful over time and thus continually increase the gap between themselves and those who have not been as successful? After all, they would be using the same talents, efforts, and self-discipline that made them more successful in the first place.

Of course the disparity between the rich and the poor is always going to increase in a free society. But that, of and by itself, does not harm anyone. The only problem is the one caused by the angry Retrogressive who has unilaterally decided that such a gap isn't "fair." Which, of course, is merely his subjective opinion. What the Retrogressive does not understand is that the rich person's success does not in any way prevent the poor person from becoming financially successful. The Constitution does not guarantee his success, but it does guarantee him the right to *pursue* his success. This right—for him to succeed or fail on his own merits—has nothing whatsoever to do with anyone else's right to do the same thing. Remember, there is no single fixed pie. In a free society, everyone is free to bake his *own* pie.

Thus, I don't think of the increasing gap between the rich and the poor as fair *or* unfair. It's simply a reality. Why *shouldn't* a person be allowed to become as successful as his talents and hard work will make him, so long as he achieves his success on a noncoercive basis? While it may be interesting to muse on the success of one person as compared to that of another, such success has no moral or practical relevance except to the Retrogressive, who insists on using it as an excuse to play Robin Hood.

Of course, in reality, today's so-called poor are living better than their parents and grandparents could have ever imagined just forty or fifty years ago. The U.S. government's own Census Bureau's statistics confirm this reality. Average-income figures show that during the Reagan years almost everyone's income rose significantly, while during the Carter years, most people got poorer. Does anyone seriously believe that voters kicked Carter out of office and gave Reagan two landslide victories because they were better off under Carter and worse off under Reagan?

When Entrepreneurs can reap financial rewards by providing better goods and services to others, they are motivated to work harder and longer hours to do so. As a result, the economy prospers, jobs are created, wages increase, and everyone is better off. On the other hand, the more government interferes with this natural process, the worse off everyone is. Those who believe that a strong central government is needed to manage a nation's economy simply do not understand the awesome power of capitalism and its inherent fairness in rewarding people according to the results they produce.

If everyone would concentrate on his or her own well-being and simply ignore "the gap between the rich and the poor," we'd all be much happier and politicians would be stripped of their most precious vote-getting strategy: class warfare. I could care less about the wealth of a Donald Trump, Michael Bloomberg, or Bill Gates. None of them have made me a dime or cost me a dime (though indirectly Gates probably has contributed greatly to my success, as well as to yours and almost everyone else's, over the past thirty years or so).

All this brings to mind the infamous words of Adolf Hitler, who said, "What good fortune for government that the people do not think."

Plain and simple, the idea that successful people should not improve their financial well-being faster than others has absolutely no moral validity. The question is: Is there a politician or political commentator courageous enough to explain to the people that the constant drumbeat about the gap between the rich and the poor is political sophistry at its worst? If so, he's been in hiding for a very long time.

The government has the authority to create rights.

A human being is a creature of infinite desires, and it is quite normal to want to fulfill as many of those desires as possible. However, he is aware that merely telling people that he wants something is not likely to produce results. To overcome this problem, it has become popular to claim that whatever one desires is a "need." The transformation of a desire into a need is an integral component of the Retrogressive's redistribution-of-wealth strategy.

Need, quite obviously, is a subjective word; i.e., it is but an opinion. I may think that I need a Rolls-Royce; you may think I need a bicycle. Neither of us is right or wrong; we merely have a difference of opinion.

But my *desire* for a Rolls-Royce is another matter; there is no opinion involved there. If I desire a Rolls-Royce, that's my business. It becomes your business only if I arbitrarily decide that you have an obligation to buy it for me, on the grounds that it's a "need" and that I am therefore "entitled" to it.

The fact that I may call my desire for a Rolls-Royce a *need* is, of course, semantic nonsense. I may just as well call it a wart, because regardless of what word I assign to it, I still have no moral right to force you to help me acquire it just because I happen to want it.

However, this camouflage is only the first step in the semantics game that is part and parcel of the Retrogressive's redistribution-of-wealth scheme. The second step involves the clever elevation of "needs" to "rights." All Western cultures now accept the belief that every individual has a right to an education, a right to a "good" job, a right to a "minimum" wage, a right to "decent" housing, a right to virtually anything that a person can establish as "society's obligation" to him. This is quite a contrast to earlier times, when most people believed that no one had a right to anything except life, liberty, and the pursuit of happiness.

Unfortunately, Western civilization has devolved to the point where the use of force and fraud can be easily justified on the grounds that such measures are necessary to make certain that people's "rights" are not violated—i.e., to make certain that their individual *desires* are fulfilled. And when all is said and done, that is what today's politics are all about. The Constitution be damned, government's number-one function has become redistribution of wealth.

There is, quite obviously, one glaring problem with the desires-to-needs-to-rights game. In order to fulfill the "rights" of one person, another person's right to liberty must be violated, because any product or service that an individual may desire must be produced by someone else. And if the product or service (or the money to purchase it) is taken from a productive citizen against his will, then that citizen's rights have been sacrificed to the desires of the person who receives the largesse. We should never forget that money for people programs comes from people!

Nevertheless, over a period of many decades, most people have come to believe in the Retrogressive's notion that elected politicians—not to mention nonelected bureaucrats—have the authority to grant, as well as take away, individual rights. These phantom rights include such things as the right to a "decent" job at a "fair" wage, the right to an "affordable home," and the right to "adequate" healthcare.

I refer to these as *phantom rights* because never did the Founding Fathers write, say, or so much as imply that government has the authority create rights for anyone. On the contrary, they made it eminently clear that our rights are granted to us by our Creator, and even those rights are limited to "life, liberty, and the pursuit of happiness."

Government-created rights defy the workings of the marketplace, where people are free to make their own choices. This puts the Entrepreneur at a decided disadvantage, because he's in the business of trying to succeed in the marketplace by marketing to prospective customers, then pleasing them with his products or services.

The whole notion of someone else's need being a right—a right that the Retrogressive views as a claim on *your* God-given right to pursue your own life, liberty, and happiness—was put in proper perspective by John C. Goodman:

To appreciate the classical liberal concept of individual rights, it is as important to understand what is being rejected as it is to understand what is being

151

asserted. To say that individuals have the right to pursue their own happiness implies that they are not obliged to pursue the happiness of others. Put differently, the right to life, liberty and the pursuit of happiness implies that people are not obligated to serve the needs, concerns, wishes and wants of others. This doesn't mean that everyone has to be selfish. It does imply that everyone has a right to be selfish.

In the classical liberal world, need is not a claim. That is, the needs, wishes, wants, feelings and desires of others are not a claim against your mind, body or property. At the time the Declaration of Independence was written, this meant that the American colonists had the right to pursue their own interests, independent of the needs of King George and the British Empire. In time, the concept was broadened—affirming each individual's right to pursue his or her own interest, despite the existence of unmet needs somewhere on the planet or even next door.

The idea that need is not a claim applies to procedural rights as well as substantive rights. Tom may feel safer if all suspicious-looking people are routinely seized and searched. But in the world of classical liberalism, Tom's need to feel safe is not a justification for initiating force against all suspicious-looking people.[6]

What makes the Retrogressive's notion of rights even more dangerous is that these artificial rights seem to be infinitely expandable. In that regard, I recall the appearance of a very angry, far-left professor by the name of Dr. Caroline Heldman on *The O'Reilly Factor* one evening. After listening to her blather incoherently about people's rights, Bill O'Reilly interrupted her and asked that she be specific and name what rights she believed every person possesses. After stumbling around a bit, she finally blurted out, "Well, one that we can all agree on is the right to life, liberty, and the pursuit of happiness." "Wow!" I thought to myself. "Maybe she recently read Thomas Paine and experienced a moral conversion."

Not quite. Heldman went on to expand on her comment by explaining that in order to have life, a person has to have free healthcare; in order to have life, a person has to have a guaranteed job that pays a "decent wage"; in order to have life, a person has to have a free education. At that point, O'Reilly cut in and admonished her to dispense with the nonsense. Artificially created rights are the logical consequence of an anything-goes society, because you can just make them up as you go along.

The Entrepreneur recognizes that he has no right to anyone else's life or property and that the only way he can achieve financial success is through the rigors of the market. He knows that his desires and subjective needs are of no interest to anyone else—especially strangers. Unfortunately, the fact that millions of people have accepted the immoral notion that their desires are rights is an enormous financial obstacle that the Entrepreneur has to deal with day in and day out, because the fulfillment of government-created rights means that valuable financial resources must be taken from him and handed to others.

And even if the recipients of the money taken from the Entrepreneur turned right around and used that money to buy his products or services, they would be buying them with the very money taken from him in the first place! That being the case, an impolite person might be tempted to say that, as a result of government's generosity with his money, the Entrepreneur ends up getting screwed.

Freedom is not about security or equality; it's about *insecurity* and *inequality*. The price of freedom is self-responsibility, and self-responsibility means that no one has a right to a job, a house, a car—no, not even healthcare. What everyone does have a right to is what he is able to earn, in a totally free market, through his own efforts—*without violating the natural rights of anyone else.*

In his book *The Liberal Mind,* Dr. Lyle H. Rossiter puts it this way:

The adult citizen's dependent attachment to government comes at an enormous price: the constant growth of the politician's power to gratify his constituents is paralleled by a constant growth in his power to dominate them. Unfortunately, the resulting decline in the citizen's freedom is gradual enough to avoid alarming them.

The Anti-entrepreneurial Holy Grail

The liberal agenda's favors seduce the people a little at a time, always playing on their regressive longings to be indulged. Favor by favor, accompanied by the constant drumbeat of entitlement propaganda, the otherwise intelligent citizen is led to an increasingly erroneous conception of the proper role of government in a free society. Like a child molester, the liberal politician grooms his constituents until their natural cautions against yielding power in exchange for favors dissolves in reassurance.

Why do people allow themselves to be so duped? . . . Despite a general tendency toward increasingly realistic perceptions of the world as they grow up, children easily acquire misconceptions about human nature and the realities of human life, about the nature of government, and about the economic, social and political processes that characterize modern societies. , , ,

Some of these misconceptions can be attributed to simple ignorance. But some of them arise from neurotic and other irrational mental processes and not from lack of knowledge per se. . . . Some are characterized by delusions of grandeur, or infantile claims to entitlement, indulgence and compensation.[7]

Translation: Americans need to grow up and stop acting like helpless, spoiled children! Inviting politicians to molest them has dire, long-term consequences.

Subtle Forms of Wealth Redistribution

When people think of redistribution of wealth, the most obvious programs come to mind—like federal funding of abortions, unemployment benefits, and food stamps. All of these—and hundreds of similar programs—are, of course, unconstitutional and immoral.

If you are adamantly against the taking of human life through abortion, it doesn't matter. You are still forced to pay for strangers to have their unborn babies killed. If you are against unemployment benefits because you believe it encourages people not to work, it doesn't matter. You are still forced to pay the living expenses of strangers who are unemployed. Ditto with food stamps.

Just to be clear here, I want to emphasize that none of this has anything whatsoever to do with your willingness to provide charitable assistance to those whom *you* deem to be in need. As I discussed earlier, being charitable and being *forced* to give—especially to causes you don't believe in—are two entirely different matters.

But putting aside the hundreds of obvious wealth-redistribution programs, most insidious of all are the programs that go virtually unchallenged by the general populace because they are subtle in nature. For example:

Social Security

Social Security is a classic example of the Retrogressive's clever strategy of getting his foot in the door, then, once a program is in place, expanding it to the point where a large segment of the public comes to depend on it. The 1935 Social Security Act, which was the centerpiece of FDR's New Deal, defied the Constitution by implying that it was the government's duty to fulfill the needs and desires of individual citizens.

Initially, it was billed as a modest program that would help a relatively small number of elderly people who were truly in need. However, once the initial funding for Social Security was established as a baseline, a new baseline emerged each year to grow it into the monster redistribution-of-wealth program it has become.

Now, people think of the benefits they receive from the program as a right. But Social Security is not a right. And it is not a trust fund that all Americans pay into, knowing that the government will invest and grow their money so it will be there to provide a cushion for them in old age. That government claim is a total fraud. The truth is that Social Security is a massive redistribution-of-wealth program that politicians use as a third-rail vote-buying scheme.

Social Security is nothing more than a tax on working people. The money taken from taxpayers is commingled with other government funds, and the government—in Bernie Madoff style—simply turns around and takes enough money from its general revenues to pay benefits to seniors.

Even when conservative politicians talk about "partially privatizing Social Security," they are still ignoring the Constitution. To speak of "privatizing Social Security" not only implies that each individual should have the right to invest his money in any way he chooses, but also implies that he *must* invest it. To force someone to invest his own money is as unconstitutional as forcing someone to purchase health insurance. If it's your money, you have a natural right to do with it as you please—which includes investing it in starting or expanding an entrepreneurial venture of your own.

Healthcare

I discussed healthcare under regulations, but, like just about every government program, it is also a method of redistributing wealth. By *healthcare*, I am referring to *all* forms of government-funded healthcare, including Medicare, Medicaid, and Obamacare (officially given the misleading title of the "Patient Protection and Affordable Care Act").

The fact that a large number of Americans favor government-run healthcare is irrelevant. *Of course* some individuals would like to have their healthcare paid for by others. That's a given. But to take money by force from some people in order to give it to them is unconstitutional—and, more important, immoral.

It's not surprising that healthcare programs are wildly popular with those on the receiving end, because, as John Stossel puts it, "People like free stuff." In the case of

Medicare, for example, the money is simply taken from working people who don't yet qualify for the program and handed (through health providers) to those who do qualify. And, along the way, billions of dollars are skimmed off the top to pay government employees and bureaucrats who administer this unconstitutional program.

The irony is that people who are against Obamacare have argued that one of its worst features is that it cuts Medicare by $500 billion. Yet, Medicare, too, *is* government-run healthcare, thus it is both unconstitutional and immoral, and outside of government's restricted powers.

As I said earlier, Obamacare was intended by Retrogressives to get their foot in the door—then, through their own arbitrary interpretation, have the program evolve into what they want it to be. They have long known that once enough people are benefiting (or think they are) from the largesse that flows from a new program, it will, of course, become popular. But the debate should never be over whether a program is or is not popular. Having the top 1 percent of income earners hand over 100 percent of their earnings to the bottom 50 percent of income earners would be popular, too. But that doesn't mean it would be legal—and certainly neither moral nor sustainable.

In a 2008 speech in the United Kingdom, Donald Berwick, Barack Obama's choice for administrator of the Centers for Medicare and Medicaid Services, stated bluntly, "Any healthcare funding plan that is just, equitable, civilized, and humane must—must—redistribute wealth from the richer among us to the poorer and the less fortunate. Excellent healthcare is, by definition, redistributional."[8]

It was quite bold of Mr. Berwick to come right out and admit that government-funded healthcare is just another redistribution-of-wealth scheme, and it was refreshing to have any debate to the contrary put to bed by, of all people, the Retrogressive at the top of the healthcare chain.

It's interesting to observe how some conservatives squirm for an answer when asked if they are not concerned about people with pre-existing conditions who have no healthcare. Of *course* they are concerned, as are most people, including myself. But the solution is not to destroy our current healthcare system and make everyone equally miserable.

Another problem is that if insurance companies are forced to insure people with pre-existing conditions, they will have to raise everyone else's rates dramatically, which is the equivalent of a transfer-of-wealth program. If people refuse to pay those increased rates, their insurance companies will go out of business. Presto: The government achieves its objective of gaining full control of healthcare.

On the other hand, if the government prevents insurance companies from raising their rates so they can afford to cover people with pre-existing conditions, those companies will go out of business because they will quickly incur unsustainable losses. Presto: Again, the government achieves its objective of gaining full control of healthcare.

The Anti-entrepreneurial Holy Grail

The solution to medical care for people with pre-existing medical conditions—and people who, for one reason or another, cannot afford medical insurance—is *private charity.* Private charity always works; government coercion never works (except for the politicians who increase their power as a result of such coercion).

As time goes on, Retrogressives will increasingly argue that if government is forced out of the healthcare business, those who can't afford medical insurance will be left to die. No one wants to see anyone die unnecessarily. But if Retrogressives are as concerned about such people as they claim to be, there should be no problem. After all, in a free society they would be free to lead the way when it comes to contributing time and money to set up and fund private charities to provide for those who they believe are in need of free healthcare.

Automaker Bailouts

It's hard to believe that just fifty years ago General Motors controlled 50 percent of the U.S. auto market (now down to about 22 percent). Who could have imagined that after the harsh consequences of Pearl Harbor, the Japanese would have the temerity to invade such U.S. heartland spots as Ohio and Tennessee with their efficiently run auto plants?

While it's popular to refer to government subsidies of "too big to fail" corporations like General Motors and

Chrysler as corporate welfare, when you drill down to the core of the matter, you realize that giving money to these automakers just to keep them alive was—and continues to be—primarily a transfer of wealth from taxpayers to the pampered *union employees* of those companies.

The marketplace—which rewards legitimate Entrepreneurs who provide competitively priced goods and services that consumers want to buy—voted General Motors and Chrysler out of business. But government used force to screw bondholders and shareholders out of their equity in those companies by preventing them from being properly liquidated. Now, they are nothing more than conduits to funnel money from taxpayers to auto workers who can be counted on to both contribute to the Democratic Party and vote Democratic.

Public Education

Public education a transfer-of-wealth program? Impossible! Doesn't every child have a right to a good education? No, he does not. However, his parents do have a right to pursue an education for him through their own efforts, which does not include the right to have the government take money from you—or, worst of all, a childless couple—to pay for that education. Regardless of how many children your neighbor has, their education is *his* responsibility, not yours.

When the Retrogressive talks about a "free education," he purposely uses a misnomer. As everyone knows, nothing in life is free. It's a noble goal to want to see every child have a good education. I, for one, certainly would like to see every child in America receive the best education possible (which, to paraphrase Karl Hess, Barry Goldwater's late speechwriter, is why I would like to see the public-education system abolished).

But how would poor people pay for their children's education in a truly free society? Answer: The same way they pay for cars, cell phones, and television sets. (Remember, 97 percent of those whom government classifies as "poor" have television sets, and 73 percent have a car.) And with government not taking billions of dollars a year from taxpaying, productive citizens to pay bloated salaries and pensions to teachers more focused on retirement than on teaching, people would have money available to contribute *voluntarily* to help educate children from underprivileged homes.

Best of all, in a free market, Entrepreneurs would rush in to service those who could not afford higher priced schools. As with all services that are regulated by marketplace realities, parents would send their children to the schools that cost the least and taught the best. Education, like everything else people desire, is a commodity. And the Entrepreneur who provides the best commodity at the lowest price always wins—provided there is no government coercion involved. Which, in turn, is always best for the consumer, be he rich or poor.

In every facet of life, there's a Walmart and there's a Saks Fifth Avenue. They service different segments of the market, and both are successful because their customers are happy with their products, their service, and their prices. A private-education system based on the profit motive would operate in the exact same fashion.

Government Jobs Programs

Since the government has no resources of its own, when it "creates" a job, it simply puts someone to work on a project for which there is little or no demand in the marketplace. The money to pay the person who performs the job must come from newly printed dollars, borrowing, or taxing. All of which makes it harder for the legitimate job creators— Entrepreneurs—to create real jobs, because they have fewer resources at their disposal.

The fact is that it's impossible for government jobs programs to "stimulate the economy." It doesn't matter whether you call a new program a "stimulus package," a "jobs bill," or a banana, the result is the same—a negative impact on the economy. Resources squandered by the government are resources that are not available to the Entrepreneur to create products and services that consumers actually want, which is how *real* jobs are created.

Free Stuff

In the simplest of terms, redistribution-of-wealth programs are nothing more than bribery—a way for those who aspire to power to buy off various groups of voters with their neighbors' property. This approach is not unique to America. It has been practiced many times, in many countries, throughout the ages.

Will Durant, in *Caesar and Christ,* explained how, in 494 BC, large numbers of Rome's common folk in effect went on strike, proceeding to the Sacred Mount on the river Anio, just outside of the city. They insisted that they would not work or fight for Rome until certain demands were met, one of the most important being for their debts to be canceled or reduced.

The Roman Senate finally agreed to their demands, thus beginning a long and familiar history of governments and producing classes yielding to the demands of the masses. From that point on, a continuous stream of Roman leaders, including Spurius Cassius (486 BC), Spurius Maelius (439 BC), and Marcus Manlius (384 BC), tried to distribute wheat, land, and other commodities to the "poor" in exchange for their support.[9]

How does the American way of life fit in with the historical realities of class warfare? Those who covet what is not theirs and who have been brainwashed through the government's mass-education programs become experts at the ballot-box game. As a result, they no longer wait to be bought off. Instead, they begin to dictate the terms of the buyoff by lynching their neighbors through the political system. And in exchange for political power, politicians willingly agree to carry out these lynchings.

So, when the electorate overwhelmingly said "No!" in the 2010 elections to more government spending, the backlash was predictable. Those on the receiving end of a redistribution-of-wealth culture like things just the way they are, thank you.

I fully understand that people like free stuff, which is why government programs that give lots of people lots of goodies are always popular. That human failing, however, is irrelevant in the face of both Natural Law and the Constitution. It can't be repeated too often: It is not the government's job to fulfill the needs and desires of individuals. On the contrary, the chief purpose of the Constitution is to put *restraints* on the government. By no stretch of the Constitution is it the government's job to redistribute wealth. The government's only valid role is that of bodyguard.

The fact is that plunder is not a right. It is a criminal activity. Which means that all elected officials and non-elected bureaucrats who take money from productive, tax-paying citizens and transfer it to certain groups of people under the guise of its being a right are criminals. Frederic Bastiat summed up the problem we now face in the United States and all Western countries when he said:

When plunder is organized by law for the profit of those who make the law, all the plundered classes try somehow to enter—by peaceful or revolutionary means—into the making of laws. According to their degree of enlightenment, these plundered classes may propose one of two entirely different purposes when they attempt to attain political power: Either they may wish to stop lawful plunder, or they may wish to share in it.[10]

As any student of human nature could have predicted, a majority of the population has chosen to share in our legalized system of plunder as opposed to allowing the Entrepreneur to create jobs so people could actually work for a living. Of course, to tell the recipient of a forced buyoff that his little game of "my desires are rights" is immoral would be political suicide. Have you ever heard even the most conservative elected official tell his constituents that the financial problems of the United States are a direct result of the covetousness of voters?

Unfortunately, there is an inherent desire in men to prosper without effort, and it is the repression of this desire, both voluntarily and through the institution of laws, that makes a civilized society civilized. It would therefore be justifiable to say that the United States can no longer be considered a civilized society.

Fortunately, not everyone has bought into the absurdity that they can live the good life without working. As Dr. Rossiter explains:

[In] providing for his own material and interpersonal well-being, and the well-being for those for whom he

has assumed responsibility, the competent person has no need of parental services. While always humanly fallible and vulnerable, and always subject to failure and loss, his efforts to run his life through his own initiative ordinarily suffice well enough and are personally satisfying in their own right.

In particular, he has no need or desire for the government to assume a task that he is able to perform for himself, with or without the assistance of others. Beyond certain very limited though critical government functions, such as the protection of property and contract rights, military defense against other nations, and the coordination of those relatively few matters best regulated as public goods, the competent man desires only to be let alone by the government in order that he may continue to live his life as he chooses—while he honors the rights of others to do the same.[11]

Having been sold on the childish illusion that their desires should be fulfilled through the use of force, nonproducers desperately fear any proposed change in the lynch-mob-rule structure that has, for decades, filled their consumption cup to the brim. Sadly, these people think it is to their advantage to perpetuate the immoral redistribution system that has become so firmly entrenched in our culture, because they ignorantly believe they benefit from it.

But it is not just the masses that stand in the way of a return to a moral society. As paradoxical as it may seem, big business often supports the plunder system. Why? Because major corporations, having adjusted their business models, financial planning, product designs, and marketing strategies to a theft-is-moral society, have a major stake in seeing to it that the rules of the game remain unchanged.

Were it not for continued inflation, taxation, government subsidies, plunder laws, and other forms of government intervention in the economy, many large companies would cease to exist. At the very least, they would cease to be large.

Take the banking industry. Banks benefit directly from the government's redistribution schemes, because the more leeway they are given to inflate their supply of paper money, the more they can "earn" (in interest on money that does not actually exist). But bankers are not alone in siphoning off the earnings of producers. Entire industries have grown up on a foundation of monetary inflation and redistribution laws.

Where would Las Vegas be today if a whole generation of Americans had not been made to feel much wealthier than they are? Fifty years ago, Las Vegas was a haven for well-heeled people who wanted to get away for a few days and relax. Now that the wealth has been spread around through the use of force, Las Vegas no longer caters only to those who can actually afford it, but also to people whose pockets are lined with dollars they wouldn't possess in a truly capitalistic society.

Millions of people who, only a few decades ago, would no more have thought of boarding an airplane and flying to Las Vegas to give away hundreds, or even thousands, of their dollars to the blackjack or craps tables now flock there even in the worst of times. If the United States suddenly reverted to a totally free society in which each individual could receive no more than what an employer was willing to pay him without government coercion, and if the government were taken completely out of the money business, Las Vegas would collapse overnight.

And how about the fast-food industry? Or the vacation/travel industry? For some time now, the name of the game for companies in these industries has been to gear their products and services to the masses. You don't build Ramada Inns and sell KFC chicken to "the rich." All major corporations now cater not only to the true middle class, but also to the middle class that has been artificially created by government redistribution programs.

The Retrogressive argues that, regardless of its shortcomings, the end (helping the poor) justifies the means (redistributing wealth). But all evidence leads to the contrary conclusion. While they may have flat-screen TVs, iPads, and cell phones, studies show that those who are the most economically challenged are worse off now, in more important ways than material possessions, than before Lyndon Johnson thrust the Great Society upon us. Consider:

- During the civil rights movement of the 1960s, 70 percent of black families were intact, with husband and wife together. Today, 60 percent of black children grow up in fatherless homes.

- Seventy percent of black babies are born to unwed mothers.

- More than three hundred thousand black babies are aborted annually.

- Eight hundred thousand black men are in jail or prison.

- Fifty percent of new AIDS cases are in the black community.

- Almost half of young black men in America's cities are neither working nor in school.[12]

In addition, as America's decline has accelerated, its legal system has been turned upside-down as well. It now sanctions—and enforces—the taking of others' property. In fact, wealth without work is now encouraged by the governments of all Western countries. Since it is only natural for men to want to avoid hardship, while at the same time enjoying the good things in life, the masses are not about to let go of their something-for-nothing cornucopia without a fight.

Still, the government has no constitutional or moral authority to implement *any* wealth-transfer program, no matter how worthy some people may believe it to be. Unfortunately, the idea that a politician's self-proclaimed compassion gives him the right to take the property of law-abiding citizens and give it to others is a perversity that has come to be accepted by a large percentage of the population.

The truth, of course, is that the so-called poor have more opportunity under capitalism than any other system. The reason for this is self-evident: It's because they are *free*—free to rise above their current station in life. As the stories of countless rags-to-riches Entrepreneurs have demonstrated, when a person is free, anything is possible.

Nevertheless, millions of people still yearn to push the concept of redistribution of wealth to its logical conclusion: communism.

The Last Communist

For years, the clueless media loved to refer to Fidel Castro as "the last communist." This perplexed me no end, because history has made it clear that there's no reason to believe that communism, which has existed since man's earliest days on this planet, will ever cease to exist.

A belief in communism is a mental disorder of sorts. Through education, logic, and a sound moral structure, a majority of Americans have been able to overcome its serpentlike temptation of cradle-to-grave security for the better part of two centuries. But early man had no formal education, and, one would assume, no time to reflect on philosophical—and certainly not ideological—issues.

The evidence suggests that savages lived communal lives where the individual was sacrificed to the "collective good." Often, this even resulted in cannibalism. Satisfying one's appetite by munching on a fellow tribe member's arm must have seemed quite natural to men who, like animals, spent most of their time hunting for food. But with the advent of the Agrarian Revolution in the Neolithic Age, civilization advanced and the individual gradually gained in importance.

In more modern times, after the fall of the Soviet Union and the Berlin Wall, communism became passé to the average person. As the economy boomed in the United States and other Western countries, many of those who were most susceptible to the allure of the communist fantasy of wealth without work became distracted by the good life handed to them by their thriving semicapitalistic systems.

Nevertheless, communism has never been completely eradicated, because a significant percentage of any country's population simply cannot resist the idea of divvying up the wealth. Thus, throughout the twentieth century, communism reared its ugly head in such disparate places as Russia, North Korea, Vietnam, Cambodia, Mozambique, and, in our own hemisphere, Cuba. Now, in the twenty-first century, it's starting to take hold in Venezuela under Hugo Chávez, with the United States clearly the next big target of those who yearn for "social justice" (i.e., total redistribution of wealth).

So what, exactly, is communism? It is defined as "a theory advocating elimination of private property; a system in which goods are owned in common and are available to all as needed; a totalitarian system in which a single authoritarian party controls state-owned means of production with the professed aim of establishing a stateless society; a final stage of society in Marxist theory in which the state has withered away and economic goods are distributed equally." Sounds like a lot of fun, doesn't it?

But what about socialism? Isn't socialism a good compromise between capitalism and communism? If you take the trouble to look it up, you'll find that the only significant difference between socialism and communism is that socialism is referred to as "a transitional stage of society between capitalism and communism." Which means, according to *Newsweek* ("We Are All Socialists Now"), that the United States is well on its way to communism.

Many countries, particularly in Europe, try to stop at socialism and not finish the journey to pure communism. They do this because they realize that under socialism, politicians can still rely on the remnants of capitalism to prop up their redistribution schemes. And for a while, it works. However, it is the nature of "democracies" to continually move to the left, and for the masses to scoff at the notion that their country is on its way to communism.

One of the few things John Edwards was ever honest about was his view that there are two Americas. But the two Americas are not the ones he invented for political purposes. The two Americas that actually exist are the America that believes in self-responsibility, hard work, and the primacy of the individual, and another—which consists of about one-third of the U.S. population—that believes in an abstraction known as "the common good" and the fantasy of some people of living off the efforts of others.

To all those who are still living in a kumbaya dream world, hear this: There is no compromise between these two positions. Socialism must lead either to communism or a total collapse of a nation's economy. It can never lead to self-responsibility, hard work, and the primacy of the individual.

When Fidel Castro said, in 2010, that communism no longer worked in Cuba, it was a stunning admission on his part—kind of a deathbed conversion to the efficacy and morality of freedom and free markets. It was, of course, a horrific blow to the far left, particularly in the United States. Without saying the actual words, Castro was saying that it is through the efforts of the Entrepreneur, not the government, that people's lives are made better.

Here we are, hurtling full speed toward a collectivist

utopia in America, while countries like Vietnam and China are moving just as rapidly toward capitalism. State-controlled capitalism, to be sure, but, still in all, capitalism. And now, to rub insult into injury, Cuba is hinting that it is about ready to embark on a similar journey.

If I were one of the hundreds of thousands of Cuban-Americans who had to flee their homeland and leave their possessions behind, I would be very angry right now. Fifty years of oppressing an entire nation, and now Castro says communism doesn't work? Sorry, Fidel, but your deathbed enlightenment doesn't bring back all the lost family members and stolen wealth that your regime was responsible for. Nor does it bring back all those lost years for millions of Cubans who were forced to live in a police state.

Like other communist countries, Cuba will increasingly implement "reforms" that will move it more and more in the direction of freedom and free markets and start encouraging entrepreneurship. And, as with most other communist countries that have collapsed under the weight of their own systems, Fidel, brother Raúl, and their fellow thugs will slip quietly into the night and never have to answer for their crimes.

So, where does this leave the Michael Moore–Sean Penn–Oliver Stone crowd? Embarrassed? Never. The far left has a stand-pat response whenever they are confronted with yet another communist failure. They simply argue that Karl Marx's model has never been properly implemented, which is why all communist countries have failed. A convenient excuse, to be sure.

Perhaps Hugo Chávez will be the first dictator ever to figure out how to make communism work for "the people." In the meantime, the real reason every communist regime in history has brought death, enslavement, and economic disaster to its people is that communism is a political and economic system that was conceived in failure. Plain and simple, it defies human nature. People—*all* people—seek to better their existence, and it takes the brute force of a dictatorship to suppress that instinct.

The bottom line to redistribution of wealth is that it leads to an entitlement mind-set that craves—indeed, demands—ever more pie that is baked by someone else. And that, in turn, leads to everything from unemployment to hyper (or runaway) inflation to decreased freedom, all of which are an invitation to authoritarian rule. Redistribution of wealth can never have a happy ending. The bad ending can be delayed, but the longer it takes, the worse it will be.

6.

THE GAVEAD SYNDROME

When the lessons of history so clearly demonstrate that redistribution of wealth always ends badly for a nation, what could possibly motivate so many people to ignore such evidence? I believe the answer can be found in an acronym I like to refer to as GAVEAD (guilt, arrogance, victimization, envy, anger, demonization). These human character flaws are powerful drivers that cause people on the giving as well as the receiving end of the Retrogressive agenda to act on emotion rather than logic or morality.

At its worst, GAVEAD manifests itself in bloody revolutions, such as the Bolshevik Revolution in Russia in 1917 and Fidel Castro's overthrow of the Batista regime in Cuba in 1959. I know of no place or time in history when GAVEAD-inspired revolutions achieved a better, freer life for anyone who was not part of the ruling elite.

Guilt

Guilt is a mental condition often found in wealthy people, particularly on the East and West Coasts of the United States, most—but not all—of whom did not acquire their fortunes through their own efforts.

The Kennedys and Rockefellers are good examples of guilt-ridden heirs to fortunes. Even today, the descendants of Joseph P. Kennedy and John D. Rockefeller are among the biggest advocates of wealth redistribution. And the most visible guilt-ridden Rockefeller is Jay Rockefeller, long-time Retrogressive senator from West Virginia.

From a psychological point of view, it's not hard to understand why someone who has been able to live in luxury all his life without ever having to do any real work would be inclined toward feelings of guilt. The problem is that the guilt feelings of those who have inherited great wealth are usually assuaged by a desire to redistribute *your* wealth to those whom *they* deem to be in need.

From Bobby to Teddy, and now in some of their most vile progeny, we see this phenomenon again and again. Because these people have no idea what it's like to start and run a business, meet a payroll, and fight to keep afloat despite excessive taxation and regulation, it is understandable that they cannot relate to the Entrepreneur.

But it's not just those who inherited their wealth who are afflicted with guilt. Guilt is also prevalent in those who have come into a lot of money quickly, again without having to do any real work. If you're thinking Hollywood, you're on the right track. The main reason so many actors talk as though they have tapioca between their ears is that they have acquired enormous wealth by doing nothing more than excelling at pretending to be someone else while in front of a movie camera.

What is not as easy to understand is how some people who have actually built fortunes through entrepreneurship—through creativity and hard work—end up feeling guilty about their wealth. In this category, Warren Buffett, Ted Turner, and Bill Gates come to mind. While I got used to the guilt-inspired, Retrogressive drivel of Buffett and Turner years ago, I have been somewhat surprised to see Gates—an admirable example of the heroic Entrepreneur in so many ways—lurch to the left.

During an interview a couple of years ago, Charlie Rose asked Gates if he felt any guilt about living in a $50 million home. Gates responded that he did sometimes feel that living such a lavish lifestyle is "a waste of resources." How, you might wonder, can the ultimate capitalist be brought down to such a cowering level?

I think we can safely give much of the credit for that feat to a far-left media that no longer reports the news, but instead works, through subtle (and sometimes not so subtle) ploys, to champion anticapitalist causes.

Consider the many times you've watched camera footage of bright-eyed, smiling youngsters happily eating their taxpayer-subsidized school lunches. Never does a "reporter" dare to suggest that perhaps even the poorest mothers could afford to make sandwiches for their own children in order to shave a billion dollars or so from the budget—or ask how children managed to survive before taxpayer-subsidized programs were instituted. The guilt-loaded, implied question is: "Would you deprive innocent little children of their minimum daily nutritional requirements?"

In his book *White Guilt,* Shelby Steele takes the guilt issue one step further by explaining that Americans are hopelessly trapped by the need to feel guilty for the sins of their fathers. Any person of color—not just black, but Arab, Latino, Asian, or other—must be coddled and handed the keys to the country (or, at the very least, to the university of his or her choice). If you don't agree, you are likely to be scorned by your friends and acquaintances and accused of lacking compassion.

A "Kinder, Gentler Nation"

If you have any doubts about how powerful media-induced guilt can be, think back on what happened as soon as Ronald Reagan left office. His successor, George Herbert Walker Bush, immediately started blathering about change, thereby beating Barack Obama to the punch by some twenty years.

When I say *immediately,* I'm talking about President Bush's inauguration address. That was when he first made an appeal for Americans to join in an effort to create a "kinder, gentler nation"—a catchphrase that the media gleefully jumped on. Never mind the fact that nations can be neither kind nor gentle. Only people can be kind and gentle—as well as nasty and harsh. But by implying that Americans were not kind and gentle, Bush also implied that they needed politicians to help them be so.

Retrogressives have always wanted more and more power to wield over the pocketbooks of American citizens. For centuries, aspiring to authoritarian rule, they had been lying in wait for the American people to display any sign of weakness—particularly guilt—that would open the door for them to remake society in their own image. Of course, they never came right out and said those words. Instead, they used words like *liberalism* (which once stood for libertarianism) and *progressivism,* because they realized that the only way they could attain power, and hold on to it, would be to camouflage their true objectives.

But perhaps the biggest problem in this regard is that for decades, Republicans have allowed their Democratic pals to make up the rules of the game. Their mantra has long been: We must show Democrats we are reasonable, civil people who are willing to "reach across the aisle" and "compromise." In other words, their desire for popularity trumps morality.

Finally, in 2001, with the country still reeling from Father George's kinder, gentler nation talk, along came Son George, who, immediately after taking office, started blathering about a weird abstraction he called "compassionate conservatism." RINOs (Republicans in Name Only) seem to have an uncontrollable propensity toward guilt—and financial suicide.

Of course, there's some pragmatism involved as well. Most politicians believe that the only way they can get elected to office, and reelected, is to prove they are "compassionate conservatives." But the term *compassionate conservatism* wrongly implies that true conservatism is not compassionate. On the contrary, the term *compassionate conservatism* is a redundancy, because true conservatism (which, as Ronald Reagan pointed out, has libertarian principles at its heart) *is* compassionate.

America doesn't need another Democratic Party. The one it has is already bankrupting and enslaving us. What it needs is a party that will stand up for freedom, and that is possible only if its members refuse to give in to unfounded feelings of guilt.

Arrogance

It's all but impossible to be a Retrogressive without possessing a great deal of arrogance. How else could someone believe he has the moral authority to create rights for others, redistribute wealth from those who earn it to those who don't, and regulate people's lives?

Meanwhile, the Entrepreneur is too busy focusing on his business objectives to even consider telling others how to live their lives. Eric Hoffer put it well when he said, "A man is likely to mind his own business when it is worth minding. When it is not, he takes his mind off his own meaningless affairs by minding other people's business."

When I think back on our country's most well-known Retrogressives, in every case their arrogance was breathtaking. As noted earlier, modern retrogressivism started with Theodore Roosevelt and his founding of the Progressive Party in 1912. Roosevelt believed that he (and whomever else he included in "we") had the right to decide if a man should be allowed to keep his own money. What a great incentive for the Entrepreneur to gamble everything he owns and work seven days a week to build a successful business![1]

Woodrow Wilson ran against Roosevelt for the presidency in 1912, accused him of being a dangerous progressive, and won. Result? Wilson immediately began implementing the most retrogressive policies in American history!

But it wasn't until Franklin D. Roosevelt took the oath of office in 1933 that a fundamental transformation in the constitutional structure of the United States of America became apparent to all. From there, segue to Lyndon Johnson's Great Society and, forty years later, Barack Obama's hope and change, and that transformation is on the verge of becoming permanent.

The Retrogressive often attempts to mask his arrogance by trying to give the impression that he spends a good deal of his time down in the trenches with the poor. Has there ever been a more shameless example of this than the despicable John Edwards appearing on the evening news, clad in overalls, shovel in hand, pretending to be seriously helping Katrina victims? Or Jimmy Carter mugging for the cameras in the Bronx some years ago, pretending to be helping poor black folks restore run-down buildings?

Anyone who would use the less fortunate among us as props to advance his own political agenda displays arrogance at its worst. Robert F. Kennedy was a master of magnanimity, even while living a life of lies and immoral behavior to the bitter end. Then there was brother Ted and the Chappaquiddick incident that killed Mary Jo Kopechne, Joseph P. Kennedy II's audacity in trying to get his *twelve-year marriage* to Sheila Rauch annulled (which he initially succeeded in doing, until the Vatican later reversed the decision), and, of course, John F. Kennedy's serial affairs. But let's not get started on the Kennedy clan. Whole books have already been written on their arrogant, hypocritical, "above the law" behavior.

Of and by itself, arrogance, while certainly not an attractive trait, would not be a problem for those of us who make it a habit to mind our own business. The problem is that the Retrogressive's arrogance is intertwined with his desire to remake the world in his own image by modifying human behavior. The late B. F. Skinner, collectivist psychologist and social theorist, spent his life searching for a scientific way to repress the human instinct to better one's existence. Perhaps without being conscious of it, Skinner, by focusing on the modification of human behavior, inadvertently acknowledged that self-interest is a normal human characteristic. Which is why force must be used to get people to take actions they do not believe to be in their own self-interest.

Those in power can use a variety of methods to get people to repress their desire to better themselves. It may start with simple coercion. If that doesn't work, it may evolve into a "nudge" (to use one of legal scholar Cass Sunstein's more ominous word choices). But, ultimately, if those who want to change people's behavior are serious about their task, extreme force, or violence, is necessary.

Victimization

The Entrepreneur never sees himself as a victim, because he recognizes that it's counterproductive. He knows that if you come from a poverty-stricken background, it is not inevitable that you will go through life poor. He knows that if you are born with a serious physical handicap, it is not inevitable that you will never be able to accomplish great things. He knows that no matter how many times you fail, it is not inevitable that you will continue to fail.

By contrast, millions of people in the Western world, indoctrinated by Retrogressive teachers and the mainstream media from an early age, step into the adult world fully prepared to see themselves as victims at the first sign of adversity. It's a mind-set that can become so ingrained in an individual's thinking that he can spend his entire life stuck in the victimization trap—which is precisely what most politicians want.

Such a person feels that the deck has been stacked against him. He sees himself as a helpless victim of an unjust world, and thus has no incentive to take action to try to improve his lot in life. He is doomed, at best, to mediocrity; at worst, to total failure. And, worst of all, to reliance on government's redistribution-of-wealth largesse for survival.

The victimization trap—set by vote-hungry politicians, self-anointed crusade leaders, rabble-rousing community organizers, and shameless legal hucksters operating under the respectable-sounding title of "personal injury attorney"—preys on human frailties, leading people to harbor the poisonous belief that material gain without work is not only possible, but justifiable. Victimization is a mind-set that makes it easy to justify the violation of others' rights in order to satisfy one's personal desires.

The acceleration of the concept of victimization has reached such grotesque proportions in Western society that it gives virtually everyone a reason to be labeled a victim, and nothing deadens the soul quite like victimization. In this respect, perhaps the ultimate manifestation of the victimization trap is the notion of reparations for black Americans. Self-anointed black "leaders" who shamelessly perpetrate this cruel hoax on the black community are the only ones who end up profiting from the mischief they create. In his eye-opening book *Scam,* Reverend Jesse Lee Peterson, who is black, bluntly summed up the reparations hoax this way:

Who will pay for reparations? I'll tell you who it will be. It will be people who don't have a racist bone in their bodies. It will be people who immigrated to this country after the Civil War. It will be people struggling to support a family. It will not be the slave owners; they're all dead. It will not be the Klansmen; most of those that are still around are so poor and backward they don't make enough money to pay the federal income taxes that will help bankroll a reparations deal.

Those who will pay for the problem will be those who never had anything to do with it. . . . White Americans are not guilty of the sins of the past, and they must be careful not to fall to the anger of these socialist, destructive black leaders who want to racially divide and conquer us. Black Americans must drop their anger and realize that it is not the white American who is causing their destruction but their own so-called leaders, whose evil machinations know no end.[2]

This kind of thinking is anathema to the Retrogressive, who, though overt racism is pretty much a thing of the past in the United States, is obsessively focused on righting past injustices. But the black Entrepreneur is disengaged from the notion that he deserves special treatment from people who have done him no harm. He is also disengaged from the self-defeating notion that he needs government help to succeed. He recognizes that he is not living in antebellum America but in twenty-first-century America, where he has access to endless opportunities. In this day and age, he realizes that no one needs a bushel full of artificial rights to achieve his goals.

Had Frederick Douglass, one of America's earliest black heroes and an advisor to President Lincoln during the Civil War, lived in our time, he undoubtedly would have been appalled by today's Retrogressives. He addressed the so-called Negro question this way:

Everybody has asked the question . . . "What shall we do with the Negro?" I have had but one answer from the beginning. Do nothing with us! Your doing with us has already played the mischief with us. Do nothing with us! If the apples will not remain on the tree of their own strength, if they are wormeaten at the core, if they are early ripe and disposed to fall, let them fall! I am not for tying or fastening them on the tree in any way, except by nature's plan, and if they will not stay there, let them fall. And if the Negro cannot stand on his own legs, let him fall also. All I ask is, give him a chance to stand on his own legs! Let him alone![3]

There's nothing that upsets the Retrogressive more than black conservatives who believe that blacks should be left alone to succeed or fail on their own merits. It is they, not blacks who spend their time agitating through "community organizing," picketing, and protesting, who are heroes—heroes whom young blacks should be encouraged to emulate.

Blacks who still buy into the drama of victimization—who demand endless apologies, special treatment for past injustices, and never-ending free goodies from the government—seem determined to make certain that white guilt remains alive and well in perpetuity. They don't *want* to move on.

But the black Entrepreneur is too busy getting ahead in life to allow racism, perceived or real, to slow him down. Thus, he ignores vote-hungry politicians, self-anointed crusade leaders, and other social charlatans who encourage group victimization. The Retrogressive, on the other hand, fully realizes that indoctrination and the lack of a good education (thanks to the public-school system) is the best way to keep blacks on (what political commentator Star Parker has referred to as) "Uncle Sam's Plantation"— the servitude that millions of blacks have suffered through as a courtesy of Lyndon Johnson's Great Society.

In Loren Eiseley's 1946 classic, *The Immense Journey*, he said, "The door to the past is a strange door. It swings open and things pass through it, but they pass in one direction only."[4] In other words, the past is the past, and you have only two choices: Move forward or live a life of stagnation. The wise Entrepreneur—be he white or black—knows that the only rational choice is to forget about the past and keep opening new doors to the future.

The truth that the Retrogressive does not want to face up to is that an individual, regardless of color, can get just about anything he wants in life—easier, faster, and in far greater abundance—without using government force to make others give it to him. As a bonus, when an individual achieves success on his own merits, it gives him a sense of accomplishment and high self-esteem.

Sadly, millions of Americans who are caught in the victimization trap demand that the government take more and more from producers to fulfill their desires. And every dollar that flows to them is a dollar that cannot be used for entrepreneurial activities that create jobs and economic growth.

The Entrepreneur thinks as an individualist and does

not allow himself to be swept up in the hysteria of group grievances. He knows that *his* mind-set and *his* willingness to take action are what will determine *his* success. Rather than embracing the poisonous idea of victimization, the Entrepreneur turns to resourcefulness when confronted with obstacles. He recognizes that government is not the solution to his problems, but the cause—and that the best place to find solutions is in the mirror.

Envy

There is a great deal of bitterness and frustration in our world due to feelings of inadequacy and failure, and many people believe they can quell their bitterness and frustration by bringing others down to their own level. Politicians are well aware of this, which is why they use envy as a political weapon to incite the masses into believing that they will somehow feel better if they can eat the rich and make everyone equally miserable.

Envy was the driving force behind America's moral revolution that began in the sixties, and it is the driving force today behind the Retrogressive's relentless march toward equality of results. And our lynch-mob system of wealth redistribution has been exacerbated by the liberal media, which continually incite the public's envy.

Envy is what the Cloward-Piven strategy is all about. That strategy, as taught back in the sixties by Columbia University activists Frances Fox Piven and her late husband, Richard Cloward, is to push as many people as possible onto the welfare rolls and thereby overwhelm the system and collapse the economy. The welfare system would then be replaced by a guaranteed minimum income for everyone. Today, nearing eighty years of age, Piven is still lecturing on the need to collapse the economy and seems to be increasingly advocating violence.

Envy is a vicious cycle: the more envy, the more destruction; the more destruction, the less wealth there is to buy off the envious; the less the envious receive, the more their envy is stirred. It's a closed loop that has been a major factor in creating the financial crisis we now see in virtually every facet of our economy.

Throughout history, envy (along with its first cousin, covetousness) has resulted in an endless stream of "people's" revolutions, but always to no avail. Revolutions may have a romantic appeal to the individual riddled with envy, but they always remind me of the words of Benjamin, the donkey, in George Orwell's classic *Animal Farm*: "Windmill or no windmill . . . life would go on as it had always gone on—that is, badly." Meaning that long after the romance of the revolution has vanished, the masses return to their normal, miserable lives.

In the bluntest of terms, history is a long and bloody story of the have-nots wanting what the haves possess. If government redistribution schemes don't get them what they want, at the very least they hope to drag the haves down to their own level of misery. In other words, the individual consumed by envy embraces a philosophy of destruction. Some people, believing they can never hope to achieve the level of success they see others enjoying, find comfort in seeing the possessions and achievements of successful people destroyed.

The reason the American Revolution succeeded was that it was based on the exact opposite philosophy—that it was a revolution based not on envy, but, rather, on liberty. It acknowledged the sanctity of the individual and his right to be free to go as far in life as his talents and efforts would take him.

Nevertheless, today's shameless politicians know that class-warfare rhetoric sells. What, exactly, does it sell? Servitude! As Tocqueville put it, "There exists also in the human heart a depraved taste for equality which impels the weak to attempt to lower the powerful to their own level, and reduces men to prefer equality in slavery to inequality with freedom."

Class warfare—warfare between the "haves" and the "have-nots"—has been a fact of life throughout recorded history, and it is certainly alive and well today. In *Animal Farm*, Orwell wrote:

> *Throughout recorded time, and probably since the end of the Neolithic Age, there have been three kinds of people in the world, the High, the Middle, and the Low. . . . The aims of these three groups are entirely irreconcilable. The aim of the High is to remain where they are. The aim of the Middle is to change places*

with the High. The aim of the Low . . . is to abolish all distinctions and create a society in which all men shall be equal.[5]

But even if one were to argue that some people at the lowest end of the income ladder are better off after so-called socialist revolutions, the reality is that such people always give up most, if not all, of their freedom in exchange for guarantees of a cheap roof over their heads and a minimal amount of food each day.

What usually happens in a successful revolution is that the doors of elitism swing open and a small number of populist leaders rush to take their places inside and stake their claim to being part of the new upper class. As Alvin Toffler describes it in *The Third Wave*:

Time and again during the past three hundred years, in one country after another, rebels and reformers have attempted to storm the walls of power, to build a new society based on social justice and political equality. Temporarily, such movements have seized the emotions of millions with promises of freedom. Revolutionists have even managed, now and then, to topple a regime. Yet each time the ultimate outcome was the same. Each time the rebels recreated, under their own flag, a similar structure of sub-elites, elites, and super-elites.[6]

Will and Ariel Durant observed pretty much the same phenomenon:

> *Violent revolutions do not so much redistribute wealth as destroy it. There may be a redivision of the land, but the natural inequality of men soon recreates an inequality of possessions and privileges, and raises to power a new minority with essentially the same instincts as in the old.*[7]

In other words, in revolutions based on redistribution of wealth, nothing much changes for the masses, no matter who controls the reins of power. But, along the way, entrepreneurship is destroyed and postrevolution nations not only end up much poorer, but their people are much less free.

Nevertheless, useful idiots (a term originally used by Lenin, then Stalin, to refer to left-wing academicians and Western sympathizers of communism) continue to carry the torch of a new revolution just around the corner that will, at long last, bring life to Karl Marx's infamous words: "From each according to his ability, to each according to his need."

Today, of course, useful idiots include the Hollywood crowd, college kids, and the totally uninformed, their heads filled with thoughts of "bread and circus" and apparently unaware that Western civilization is in danger of burning to the ground. I saw a good example of this a couple of years ago when Sean Hannity interviewed two radical college girls playing the role of useful idiots by protesting the G-20 Conference being held in Pittsburgh. They explained that they were with "Free the Planet," a University of Pittsburgh organization that wants to "make environmental change to help the planet."

At one point in the interview, Hannity asked, "Why are you against capitalism?" To which one of the girls replied, "Because it puts profit as the number-one goal and not people's well-being." Ah, yes, I remember how determined Mao, Stalin, Pol Pot, and Ho Chi Minh were when it came to looking after people's well-being. I'm sure everyone in their countries misses the good old days.

Finally, Hannity asked one of the girls, "Do you support government-run redistribution of wealth?" to which she answered, "I support people-run redistribution of wealth." "How do you have people run redistribution of wealth?" asked Hannity.

"You tax them," answered his self-assured, youthful guest. She went on to note that if you divide the wealth in the country up equally, every citizen would receive $44,000 per year. (Hannity showed a lot of restraint by sparing her the embarrassment of asking where the $44,000 per person would come from if producers lost their motivation to produce.)

The capper, though, was when the girl said, angrily, "Tell me why someone ever would need to make more than $500,000 a year."[8] Sounded like she was lobbying for the job of Wealth Redistribution Czar. Perhaps Envy Czar would be even more appropriate.

Anger

From Karl Marx to Vladimir Lenin, from Andy Stern to Richard Trumka, communists have long used the wrong word in spouting their favorite slogan. It's not the *workers* of the world whom they would like you to believe they're uniting; it is the *parasites* of the world. And, make no mistake about it, hell hath no fury like a parasite scorned.

Just ask any politician in Spain or Greece—or Wisconsin! As a country moves toward socialism, the Entrepreneur produces less and less while the masses demand more and more. Their position is straightforward: "We don't give a damn if you don't have enough money to pay our entitlements. We want them anyway!"

Spoiled parasites are in a perpetual state of anger, but they take their anger to a new level whenever their host runs out of money and their freeloading party is in danger of coming to an end. That's when the communists, community organizers, and union thugs and bosses begin to beat the war drums. Violence is *always* an option for the Retrogressive if that's what it takes for him to achieve his immoral ends.

Saul Alinsky was very aware of the realities of Retrogressive anger when he said:

The fact is that it is not man's "better nature" but his self-interest that demands that he be his brother's keeper. We now live in a world where no man can have a loaf of bread while his neighbor has none. If he does not share his bread, he dare not sleep, for his neighbor will kill him. To eat and sleep in safety man must do the right thing, if for seemingly the wrong reasons, and be in practice his brother's keeper.

I believe that man is about to learn that the most practical life is the moral life and that the moral life is the only road to survival. He is beginning to learn that he will either share part of his material wealth or lose it all; that he will respect and learn to live with other political ideologies if he wants civilization to go on. This is the kind of argument that man's actual experience equips him to understand and accept. This is the low road to morality. There is no other.[9]

What a remarkably convoluted thought: *The only road to morality is to recognize that you must share your wealth or risk having it taken from you by force—or even being killed!*

Alinsky's words remind me of something that the late and liberal Bennett Cerf, one-time president of Random House, Inc., is purported to have said. As related by Nathaniel Branden in his book *Judgment Day: My Years with Ayn Rand,* Cerf candidly told him, "You have to throw welfare programs at people—like throwing meat to a pack of wolves—even if the programs don't accomplish their alleged purpose and even if they're morally wrong."

When Branden asked Cerf why, he whispered, "Because otherwise they'll kill you. The masses. They hate intelligence. They're envious of ability. They resent wealth. You've got to throw them something, so they'll let us live." [10]

To be sure, the masses do want meat. Marie Antoinette suggested cake, and discovered that her joke wasn't appreciated. A lack of meat also spawned the Bolshevik Revolution in Russia. And the masses aren't averse to rising up against anyone or anything else that threatens to keep them from their meat.

Today, of course, raw meat is out. People have become spoiled. Politicians now have to promise to cook the meat to everyone's personal taste—from rare to well done. And meat is now a metaphor for all kinds of goodies, such as vacations in Las Vegas and electronic toys from China. Keep the electronic toys coming, keep increasing credit card limits, and who knows how long the inevitable can be postponed? The inevitable I'm referring to is a deflationary or runaway-inflation depression that would dramatically increase the anger of an already very angry public.

There's no question in my mind that both Alinsky and Cerf were right in their assessments of why you have no choice but to "share" some of your possessions. But to refer to it as the "low road to morality" is preposterous. It is, in fact, a no-road to morality. Giving up any part of one's wealth out of fear is *immoral*.

When a thief has a gun pointed at your head, you give him your wallet because you don't want to end up dead. The only morality involved is the *immorality* of the thief. Nevertheless, both Alinsky and Cerf were right: As has been amply demonstrated throughout history, the masses will resort to killing if they are angry enough. And those Americans currently in the Retrogressive camp are now very angry—and will be even more so if Obama and his Retrogressive allies in Congress get thrown out of office in 2012.

Easy credit, the dramatic expansion of Fannie Mae and Freddie Mac, and, above all, the technology explosion of the eighties and nineties gave the middle class a lifestyle that only the rich had enjoyed just a few decades earlier. It's pretty hard to get people excited about a revolution when they're relaxing in the backyards of their suburban homes, grilling steaks on the barbecue, and watching the kids splash around in their ten by twenty foot swimming pools.

Convincing such folks that they were being exploited by "the rich" was a very tough sell for the Retrogressive during the prolonged false-prosperity years. There simply wasn't a lot of enthusiasm for revolution. But it was impossible to indefinitely hide what was, in reality, an invisible depression. Those pesky universal laws have a way of showing up when you least expect them, and when they finally did, false-prosperity addicts were ill prepared to deal with them. Result: ever-increasing, unadulterated anger.

In 2007, as economic reality began to set in and

unravel the false-prosperity that millions of people had come to view as a right, it opened the door for the perfect Saul Alinsky disciple to rise from the down-and-dirty community-organizing industry on the mean streets of Chicago to the pinnacle of power in the nation's capital.

To tens of millions of people who were witnessing the house-of-cards good life collapse before their very eyes, the word "change" was like a life preserver being thrown to a drowning man. No time to think about the kind of change this inexperienced, arrogant, silver-tongued kid from Kenya was talking about. To the false-prosperity addict, any kind of change was better than watching the good life slip away.

Down with capitalism, entrepreneurship, and "the rich." From the standpoint of the Retrogressive, it was the perfect time for an ultra-angry, über-radical young community organizer to move stealthily into the White House. (The foundations of Barack Obama's glaring anger are well documented by Dinesh D'Souza in his book *The Roots of Obama's Rage,* as is his Marxist background in Stanley Kurtz's excellent work *Radical-in-Chief.*)

As the abandoned son of an alcoholic polygamist and self-avowed communist from Kenya, Obama had every reason to be angry at Western colonialists, just as his father was. In fact, because Obama's mother encouraged him to follow in his father's footsteps, D'Souza is right on target when he says that, in effect, the United States "is being governed according to the dreams of a Luo tribesman of the 1950s—a polygamist who abandoned his wives, drank himself into stupors, and bounced around on two iron legs . . . raging against the world for denying him the realization of his anti-colonial ambitions."[11]

Demonization

If you want people to be angry, it's much easier to accomplish that objective if you give them a devil to focus on—someone or something that they can be made to believe is the cause of their problems. As Eric Hoffer pointed out in his classic *The True Believer,* all mass movements require a villain. For Hitler, it was the Jews. For much of the Muslim world, the devils are Israel and the United States.

But for today's Retrogressive to get maximum anger from his army of useful idiots, he knows it is much easier to point to villains such as Entrepreneurs, "big oil," Wall Street, George W. Bush, "extremist" Tea Party people, Republican state governors, the Koch brothers . . . there is no shortage of people and groups to demonize.

The easiest demonization target of all for the Retrogressive is an abstract group known for centuries as "the rich." In an interview with GRITtv, wealthy communist Michael Moore told Laura Flanders, with a perfectly straight face:

There is only so much cash. . . . What's happened is that we've allowed a vast majority of that cash to be concentrated in the hands of just a few people. . . .

They're sitting on the money, they're using it for their own—they're putting it someplace else with no interest in helping you with your life, with that money. We've allowed them to take that. That's not theirs, that's a national resource, that's ours.[12]

Moore has made a living off demonization, however hypocritical his words may be. He epitomizes the Retrogressive who loves to blather incessantly about the billions of dollars in "windfall profits" earned by major corporations (especially oil companies), vilifying those who call for lower taxes and less government regulation and pointing an accusing finger at "loopholes" used by "the rich." Through such intimidating demonization tactics, it's not uncommon for capitalist "devils" to be driven to rehabilitate themselves and convert—out of fear or guilt, or both—to retrogressivism.

The Retrogressive media are all too happy to help in the creation of scapegoats with their implicit, poisonous message: "There is only so much wealth that exists on this earth [again, the Michelle Pie falsehood], and you are being deprived of your 'fair share' by greedy people who have far more than they need." Presto! Just like that, the angry parasite is given an outlet for his frustration and anger. Oh, how good it feels to hate! Class-warfare rhetoric focused on demonizing individuals or groups is the heart and soul of Marxism, and it's a phenomenon that feeds on itself and ultimately takes on a life of its own.

Hollywood, too, plays the demonization card over and over again. Going all the way back to the sixties, the message of the cult film *The Graduate* was that those hypocritical, materialistic, phony Entrepreneurs who built businesses and made their way to the suburbs are a bunch of evil drunks and adulterers. More recently, far-left film-maker James Cameron has given us two over-the-top blockbuster, Retrogressive films, *Titanic* and *Avatar*.

Titanic bordered on comedy, with the wealthy people in first class frantically trying to save their hides as crewmen locked the riffraff in their quarters below so they wouldn't get any ideas about trying to get into the scarce lifeboats. Boo capitalists!

Avatar was even less subtle, giving mental orgasms to Retrogressive viewers as they watched evil humans try to strip a precious mineral called unobtanium from Pandora, a lush moon of a gas giant in the Alpha Centauri star system. Their activities threatened the existence of a local tribe of Na'vi—a humanoid species indigenous to Pandora.[13] To put it mildly, it was over the top even for a far-left zealot like Cameron.

The truth is all-powerful, and it bugs the hell out of the Retrogressive. And the truth is that much of the anger harbored by the far left is a result of not having legitimate moral or rational arguments for their antifreedom viewpoint. Whether the anger be guilt-based or envy-based, it's always there . . . always advocating the use of force against individuals with dissenting views.

To give rational thought to an issue is difficult for the

Retrogressive, because he is focused on his own utopian view of the world. This is why he can never explain why anyone has a right to take the fruits of someone's labor and give it to others. Lacking factual arguments, he thus chooses to speak in abstract terms such as "social justice," "the common good," and "shared prosperity," while never failing to point his finger at "the rich." After all, it's so much easier than thinking.

Bertrand Russell summed it up well when he said:

> *Men fear thought as they fear nothing else on earth— more than ruin, more even than death. Thought . . . is merciless to privilege, established institutions, and comfortable habits; thought is . . . indifferent to authority, careless of the well-tried wisdom of the ages. Thought looks into the pit of hell and is not afraid.*[14]

The Enemy from Within

A kind-hearted person might have a tendency to see a GAVEAD-afflicted individual as simply misguided. Even so, nature punishes those who are well-intentioned but ignorant as harshly as those who are smart but harbor bad intentions. Unfortunately, not only do such people get the government they deserve, they also drag along with them those who *aren't* riddled with GAVEAD and who don't want or deserve an omnipotent central government.

If Retrogressives are truly concerned about the poor, they would be wise to set aside their GAVEAD and demand that the government get out of the way of the Entrepreneur and give him the freedom to create, produce, and compete. In a small-government, laissez-faire environment, the Entrepreneur would not only create jobs for the poor, but offer products and services to them at prices they could afford.

In the first century BC, Marcus Tullius Cicero warned:

> *A nation can survive its fools, and even the ambitious. But it cannot survive treason from within. An enemy at the gates is less formidable, for he is known and carries his banner openly. But the traitor moves amongst those within the gate freely, his sly whispers rustling through all the alleys, heard in the very halls of government itself. For the traitor appears not a traitor; he speaks in accents familiar to his victims, and he wears their face and their arguments, he appeals to the baseness that lies deep in the hearts of all men. He rots the soul of a nation, he works secretly and unknown in the night to undermine the pillars of the city, he infects the body politic so that it can no longer resist. A murderer is less to fear. The traitor is the plague.* [15]

In twenty-first-century America, the traitor within our gates is the Retrogressive. Our government is now saturated with Retrogressive politicians and bureaucrats who view the Entrepreneur as the evil enemy because he stands in the way of their desire to control all aspects of every person's life.

At the time of the founding, Thomas Paine saw the danger of the enemy from within when he wrote, in his historic work *Common Sense*:

> *Society in every state is a blessing, but government, even in its best state, is but a necessary evil; in its worst state an intolerable one: for when we suffer, or are exposed to the same miseries by a government, which we might expect in a country without government, our calamity is heightened by reflecting that we furnish the means by which we suffer.*[16]

Today, more than ever, we should think about the words of Marcus Tullius Cicero and Thomas Paine and recognize that the enemy is not outside the gates; the enemy is *inside* the gates. And on October 2, 2010, I personally saw the enemy within our gates in action.

The weather was perfect—seventy-two degrees and sunny—for the "One Nation Working Together" rally at the Lincoln Memorial, an event sponsored by a wide variety of extremist, left-wing organizations (labor unions and self-proclaimed socialist and communist groups). As I parked my car and started walking toward the site, I wasn't sure what to expect, but I was determined to keep an open mind.

When I arrived at the rally, I estimated the size of the crowd to be somewhere between 75,000 and 150,000. Tabloid-size "newspapers" were in large supply. One, *The Militant,* featured the headline "Public education is a birth right, not a corporate profit." Another one, *Challenge: The Revolutionary Communist Newspaper of Progressive Labor Party,* sported a logo that read "Fight for Communism." Mind you, this was at a rally called "One Nation Working Together"—in the capital city of the United States of America!

Then there were the signs:

"Wages that are rightfully ours."

"We demand $$$ for jobs and education."

"The American Dream promises a free education."

"Black Is Back."

"Capitalism is failing. Socialism is the answer."

At one of the many tables where books were being sold, I noted such titles as *Bolshevism, What Is Marxism, The Communist Manifesto, Four Marxist Classics,* and *Black Liberation and Socialism.*

Then there were the pamphlets, sporting such patriotic verbiage as:

"Fight for a Two-Year National Moratorium to Halt All Foreclosures and Evictions."

"Jobs for All! Public-Works Program Now!"

"Make the bosses pay for *their* crisis!"

I could fill this entire book with what I saw at that rally, but the bottom line is this: The October 2 "One Nation Working Together" event was simply a celebration of that age-old disease, class warfare. Unwittingly, the hate peddlers who promoted the event provided a public service by letting us know that they are still out there, poised and ready to bring down the American way of life—especially freedom and the free-market system.

As I walked back to my car after my short stay at the rally, the little security guard inside my brain whispered to me, "This was a reminder that America is irrevocably split into those who want to put a stop to the government's policy of redistributing wealth and those who demand that the government use force to give them even *more* of other people's wealth."

The latter group—probably about one-fourth of the U.S. population—is fully prepared to sell their souls to a totalitarian regime in exchange for the "stuff" they think they deserve. I'm not sure how they define *deserve,* but it matters not. What does matter, sadly, is that they are nothing more than pawns in a power game that has existed throughout recorded history.

Right now, roughly one-half of Americans are poised to push back and try to prevent the radical left from bringing down the curtain on capitalism, individual sovereignty, and the Western way of life. But no matter what happens in the 2012 elections, no one should be deluded into believing that the war is over. The war will *never* be over.

We are living in dangerous times, and the people

behind such events as "One Nation Working Together" are dangerous people. You cannot change them. You cannot reason with them. You cannot trust them. They lie; they steal; and, above all, they believe in the use of force. And their strength comes from unions that traffic in thuggery and thievery. With Barack Obama firmly on record (on video, on audio, and in writing) as supporting, even encouraging, their violent methods, they have become emboldened to openly cause trouble and intimidate their opposition.

Make no mistake about it, GAVEAD will always be with us. Study it . . . understand it. GAVEAD poisons not only the mind, but the soul. And it's a poison that is always there, deep inside the hearts and minds of millions of people who are waiting patiently to strike and take the civilized world back to the Dark Ages of retrogressivism.

7.

IS IT TOO LATE?

You're probably familiar with the Orwellian scene that occurred on *The Oprah Winfrey Show* in 2010, when Oprah told her audience that each of them would be receiving a new Volkswagen Beetle. As the omni-benevolent queen of mass-audience hypnotism shrieked the good news to her adoring flock, the lucky folks who had come to the studio thinking they were in for nothing more than a standard dose of mind-numbing talk-show chatter began screaming, laughing, hugging, waving their arms wildly, and, yes, crying. Some even got down on their knees, apparently to praise the almighty Goddess of Stuff who giveth free Beetles to total strangers.

I expressed my bewilderment to a friend, only to have him say, "Hey, I can understand why people would get excited about being on the receiving end of a new car. Nothing abnormal about that." Alas, he missed the point. I, too, can understand why a person would get excited about being given a new car, but this was way beyond mere excitement. It was the kind of ecstasy one might expect to see in people who have just been informed that the Messiah has returned to earth.

Following the show, Volkswagen of America CEO Jonathan Browning unwittingly provided excellent insight into the madness of the Oprah crowd when he issued a statement that said, in part, "Oprah Winfrey and the Volkswagen Beetle are two American icons, so when the Oprah show approached us with this incredible opportunity to share her Beetle experience with deserving viewers, we instantly wanted to be a part of it."

Question: What the hell is a "deserving viewer"? Is *every* viewer deserving? Of what? Why? Perhaps the reason an intelligent CEO of a major corporation would make such an idiotic statement is that he realized that the masses must be constantly told that they are deserving . . . they are entitled . . . they are, above all, "hardworking Americans"—even if they're receiving unemployment benefits!

The whole thing was reminiscent of the scene in Aldous Huxley's *Brave New World* when Mustapha Mond, the supreme government power holder, said to the awed and confused Savage from the Indian reservation, "The optimum population is modeled on the iceberg—eight ninths below the water line, one ninth above."

"And they're happy below the water line?" asked the Savage.

"Happier than above it," replied Mustapha Mond.[1]

The fact is that those shrieking people in Oprah's audience are below the water line—way below. And when you're below the water line, your mind is filled with thoughts of free stuff, today's reality-show lineup, and the latest rumors that Brett Favre will soon be attempting another comeback—provided he can get a weekly pass from the nursing home. These are the kinds of blissful thoughts that make for a happy savage.

Instant Gratification

The media are motivated by the same objective as politicians: winning votes. If people like what a news commentator has to say, they cast their votes by watching him every evening, which helps to increase his network's profits. On the other hand, if too many people do not like a news commentator, they, in effect, vote him out of a job by merely switching channels.

Obviously, then, it pays for the media to say things that are popular. And nothing is more popular than telling people that they deserve more of everything . . . that they have a right to more of everything . . . that it is the government's duty to see to it that they get more of everything. To hell with the long term. Say what sells today!

Savvy marketers, too, have picked up on the effectiveness of this strategy. A great example is a furniture store chain that is, as I write this, running nonstop television ads with voices in the background repeatedly singing the words "I want it all. I want it now." This subliminal message continues while the actors in the commercial pitch the company and its products.

The first few dozen times I saw this ad, I did what I do with most commercials—pressed the mute button on my remote control. But on one particular occasion—I guess it was just spur-of-the-moment curiosity—I left the commercial on and listened to the words that were being sung in the background. "I want it all. I want it now." I wondered how many viewers thought to ask themselves why an ad for a furniture company would play those words over and over again. You can be sure that whoever created that ad didn't pick the words randomly. After all, the object of an ad is to appeal to the prospect's desires. And in early twenty-first-century America, millions of people want it all and they want it now!

It immediately occurred to me that this one ad summed up why America now finds itself a bankrupt nation that has lost its moral foundation. Through ever-increasing government handouts and intervention in the economy, Retrogressives have led people to believe that they are entitled to everything—literally. Freddie Mac and Fannie Mae are merely symptoms of the devolution of a republic into a collectivist state, their chief function being to convert into reality the absurd notion that everyone is entitled to own a home, even if he can't afford to make the payments on it. Hard work and self-discipline—the qualities that once upon a time enabled Entrepreneurs to not only secure financial security for themselves and their children but also propel America into a position of global pre-eminence— are considered to be old-fashioned ideas. It's all about having it all and having it now.

So long as the average American was given the means to spend more than his artificially inflated income could buy, he could live in an overpriced home in the suburbs, have two new cars in his driveway, and surround himself with electronic gadgets. All this made him a very happy camper. The Retrogressive, in effect, told him, "To hell with what happens

to our offspring and the United States long term. We're all entitled to the good life, regardless of whether we can afford it."

Charades

In the 1963 film classic *Charade,* Regina Lampert (Audrey
Hepburn) asks Peter Joshua (Cary Grant) why people lie.
Joshua answers, "Usually it's because they want something.
They are afraid the truth won't get it for them."

With that in mind, it's not surprising that politicians
are champion purveyors of deception. They employ it to
win our adulation and votes, secure power, and gain access
to government perks that make it possible for them to live
like multimillionaires.

I believe that the reason so many people are able to
delude themselves for so long without seeing through the
charades that are served up to them day in and day out by
government and the media is that conventional wisdom,
myths, and fairytales tend to gain strength with age. After
all, if something has been around for a long time, there
must be some validity to it, right?

What happens is that when a preposterous story—or
even an outright lie—is repeated often enough, it acquires
"legs." Meaning that it becomes self-sustaining. And if it
attracts enough adherents, it can spread exponentially.
This is how dogma manages to evolve into fact. Through
repetition, a falsehood can be transformed into truth in
the minds of millions, and often is.

In this regard, I am reminded of something Alain de Botton wrote in *The Consolations of Philosophy*:

> *It is not only the hostility of others that may prevent us from questioning the status quo. Our will to doubt can be just as powerfully sapped by an internal sense that societal conventions must have a sound basis, even if we are not sure exactly what this may be, because they have been adhered to by a great many people for a long time. It seems implausible that our society could be gravely mistaken in its beliefs and at the same time that we would be alone in noticing the fact. We stifle our doubts and follow the flock because we cannot conceive of ourselves as pioneers of hitherto unknown, difficult truths.[2]*

Just as people get the government they deserve, they also get the charades they deserve—and *want*. That's right, most people *want* to be deluded. It feels so warm and fuzzy compared to the harshness of reality. By creating the *illusion* of freedom, so-called democratic governments are more likely to gain the support of their subjects. Give the masses enough sporting events, reality TV, and credit-card-created vacations and they can be enticed into remaining quite docile.

I recall one of Larry King's last shows when he was

interviewing one of those no-name "financial advisors" who sound as though they're all reading from the same talking points. The ever-tough Larry asked Ms. No Name what people could do to improve their deteriorating financial situation during these bad economic times. The first bit of financial advice she offered was that a person could save $200 a year by "giving up his one-bottle-of-water-a-day habit." Powerful stuff, eh?

Her second suggestion was for a person suffering financial problems to consider bringing a sandwich to work instead of going out to lunch. Sheer, unadulterated financial genius.

Then, without warning, it came—the jaw dropper. Ms. No Name went on to say that people might also "consider cutting back their entertainment to three nights a week from four." No, I'm not joking. I immediately turned to my wife and said, "Do you realize that woman, though she probably doesn't even know how to spell the word *economics,* just explained why Americans are doomed?"

Maybe I should feel embarrassed to say it, but I am obliged to admit that I've never experienced four nights of "entertainment" in any one week of my entire life! It makes me feel kind of out of it to know that my mailman may have been going out four nights a week all these years, while I've been home reading and going to bed early. But, hey, he wants it all and he wants it now.

The fact is that people are addicted to having a good time. And, besides, they're *entitled* to it. To hell with frugality. Self-delusion is essential to the American who is determined to let the good times continue to roll without regard to the economic facts of life.

So, are those of us who are productive members of society somehow immune to the consequences of the self-destructive tendencies so many of our countrymen exhibit? Would that it were so, but, in case you hadn't noticed, the Roman Empire is not with us anymore. It fell under the weight of its own charades.

Thomas Sowell once said, "Everything is new if you are ignorant of history. That is why ideas that have failed repeatedly in centuries past reappear again, under the banner of 'change,' to dazzle people and sweep them off their feet."

It is therefore not surprising that we continue to accept the charade that freedom and equality can coexist. Perhaps to some people this is a noble idea, but, unfortunately, it is not conducive to the survival of a civilization. It is simply another one of those endlessly recycled ideas that have never worked.

Animal Spirits

But what about optimism? If the average American is optimistic about the future of the economy, won't that have a positive effect on the way things turn out?

Going all the way back to the Tulip Bulb Mania in Holland in the 1630s, the madness of the crowd has always had an impact on the markets. But so long as the markets were relatively free, it was just a matter of time until economic reality set in. And when it did, bubbles created by unfounded optimism ultimately burst, while economic downturns created by unfounded pessimism (not nearly as frequent) ultimately rebounded.

In his 1936 book *The General Theory of Employment, Interest and Money,* John Maynard Keynes coined the term "animal spirits" to describe the phenomenon of economic activity that is sometimes driven by waves of optimism or pessimism. You would have thought that history would have eradicated the idea of animal spirits, but not so. In 2010, two Retrogressive economists, George Akerlof of the University of California, Berkeley, and Robert Shiller of Yale, coauthored a book titled *Animal Spirits* wherein they tried to make the case for massive government market intervention as the best way to quell pessimism and motivate people to spend—in other words, for government to use its power to deceive people into being optimistic. The far-left blog Daily Kos had this to say about the book:

With Animal Spirits we hone in [sic] on how incentives and narratives can be created to channel the human psychological factor into collectively healthy directions, and how to be aware of the fictions we tell ourselves about how we wish the world and greed and financial security worked.[3]

Honest, I'm not making up this Orwellian babble. It is, of course, the exact opposite of the truth—i.e., that government intervention in the marketplace distorts economic reality, prolongs economic downturns, and, at its worst, can lead to a total collapse of the economy.

Politicians and their lobbying pals keep trying to pump us up by telling us we're a nation of believers, and I guess to an extent they're right. Being a believer can be a good thing. Belief in coworkers who have proven themselves to be competent and trustworthy is a good thing. Belief in your family is a good thing. Belief in your own abilities is a good thing.

There's no question about it, when you have factual or experiential evidence to back it up, belief is a positive attribute. But believing in verbal gibberish and cheerleading that's camouflaged as news, believing in empty slogans, and, above all, believing in charade-dispensing politicians is precisely what has allowed the enemy from within to gain a foothold and work to destroy our nation.

Yes, we *are* a nation of believers. But, unfortunately, we believe so easily that we take seriously the words of the worst kinds of scoundrels and charlatans who continually tell us the tallest of tales.

One of the greatest propagandists of the twentieth century, Joseph Goebbels, bluntly stated: "Think of the press as a great keyboard on which the government can play." Never have we seen a greater example of this than in watching the mainstream media act, for all practical purposes, as the public-relations arm of the Obama administration.

In a free country, of course, you have a right to go on believing whatever you want to believe. But, at the same time, you should recognize that neither ignorance nor being out of touch with reality is an excuse for making wrong decisions.

The Issue Is Freedom

In the latter part of the eighteenth century, something unheard of happened in a faraway British outpost called America. The late W. Cleon Skousen called it "a miracle that changed the world." He was, of course, referring to the birth of the United States of America.

Historians have long referred to the American Revolution and subsequent birth of the United States as "the great American experiment." Could a country actually survive if its citizens declared themselves to be above the government? The idea of people having *natural* rights—given to them by God rather than by government—was unique in human history. And just as unique was the idea that those who governed would not only be elected by the people, but *their* rights would be strictly limited to those set forth in a document created by the people themselves. Specifically, the idea was that citizens would lend certain limited powers to elected officials for the purpose of protecting their lives and property. Period!

Thus, the boldest move in doing away with dictatorial government was the signing of the Declaration of

Independence. It was the colonists' way of telling their English rulers: "Enough! We hereby declare ourselves to be free." Unfortunately, from that point forward, the apparently uncontrollable urge of some of the revolutionists to govern their fellow colonists led to the creation of another document—the Constitution—which, in turn, created that most dreaded of all human inventions: the nation-state.

Nevertheless, the Constitution is a brilliant document and, I believe, well-intended. It seems clear that most of the signers saw it as a document that would protect the rights and freedom of the inhabitants of the Colonies. But human nature being what it is, a democracy (or a republic, which ultimately disintegrates into a democracy) is destined—through an "excess of democracy"—to move toward an all-powerful central government that tyrannizes its citizens. This occurs because the masses begin demanding ever more bread and circuses in exchange for freedom.

That's why the formation of the United States of America was, in every sense of the word, an experiment. And many of the Founding Fathers were skeptical about its chances of succeeding. In this vein, George Washington said that "there is a natural and necessary progression, from the extreme of anarchy to the extreme of tyranny." The French Revolution, which, ironically, was inspired by the American Revolution, was a classic example of this.

Benjamin Franklin spoke to another kind of concern when he said that "there is a natural inclination in mankind to kingly government." Throughout history, the tendency of human beings has been to willingly, or at least unthinkingly, subject themselves to a ruler or ruling class. It's no wonder that after the adjournment of the Constitutional Convention, when asked by an anonymous citizen what kind of government the Founding Fathers had created, Franklin is purported to have answered: "a republic, if you can keep it."

In writing the Constitution, the Founders worked hard to protect against a drift toward tyranny, but no document can be foolproof when it comes to protecting humans from the ravaging effects of human nature. This quickly became evident after the Constitution went into effect in the summer of 1788. It took only a decade for Congress, under John Adams, to pass the Alien and Sedition Acts of 1798, which made it a crime for anyone to criticize the government "through writing or any other shape, form, or fashion." Specifically, criticizing the president, Congress, the military, or the flag was deemed to be illegal.

This by a group of men who themselves had escaped bondage only twenty-two years earlier! Power does, indeed, corrupt. It was an audacious move by the Federalist-controlled Congress to silence the Republicans, chiefly because of their support of the French Revolution. It was, of course, in direct violation of the Bill of Rights, which clearly states, in the First Amendment, that "Congress shall make no law . . . abridging freedom of speech, or of the press."

A little more than a hundred years after the passage of the Alien and Sedition Acts of 1798, Congress, at the urging of Scoundrel in Chief Woodrow Wilson, acted again and passed the U.S. Sedition Act of 1918. Among other things, the act made it a crime to "willfully utter, print, write, or publish any disloyal, profane, scurrilous, or abusive language about the form of government of the United States, or the Constitution of the United States, or the military or naval forces of the United States."

Fast-forward to 2009. Led by the über-Retrogressive Cass Sunstein, the criminal administration in Washington began talking about infiltrating "conspiracy groups" (read Tea Party) in an effort to undermine them. (A conspiracy group is, of course, any group of people that consists of individuals who disagree with the Retrogressive policies of the current administration.) Which raises the question: Is another Alien and Sedition Act on the horizon?

More than anything else, what made America exceptional from the outset was that its people were free, and it is that freedom we are now losing at an accelerating pace. It's amazing how many people didn't see this for such a long period of time—and, worse, how many *still* do not see it.

The fact that so many people do not understand that we are losing our freedom has its roots in the false assumption that those in power actually want America to prosper. I challenge this assumption on the basis that a prosperous America would mean fewer people dependent on government help, which is anathema to the Retrogressive politician. Reality check: The agenda of those who are now at the top of the Washington food chain is to transform the United States into a collectivist utopia in which the government plans, controls, and, yes, owns everything. The vast majority of Americans are in denial about this, notwithstanding mountains of evidence to the contrary.

Since government has a monopoly on the use of force, it can crush everything that gets in the way of its main objective: power. And when I say *crush everything*, that includes marketplace realities. Government can take your money and use it to prop up the companies of its choice. It can refuse to pay its obligations or simply inflate them out of existence. Worst of all, it can silence you if you express dissatisfaction with its policies.

So, yes, the real issue is freedom, because if you have freedom, you automatically have free markets. And if you have free markets, you have entrepreneurship and a strong economy. But without freedom, the only free market is the black market, which is the only market that flourished throughout seventy years of communism in the Soviet Union and kept the country from collapsing much earlier than it did.

I get concerned whenever I hear talking heads blathering about the need for Republicans and Democrats to "come together" and show a willingness to compromise so they can "get something done." Talk about not getting it. Why would we want Republicans to "come together" with their Democratic counterparts who want bigger government, more spending, more taxes, more regulation—and less liberty for American citizens?

Those who propelled Tea Party candidates into office don't want them to *slow* the growth of government spending; they want government spending drastically *cut*. They don't want the "Bush tax cuts" extended; they want *more* tax cuts. They don't want closer oversight of the EPA; they want the EPA *defunded*—or, better yet, *closed.*

But if Republicans embraced this kind of attitude, wouldn't it cause gridlock? Yes! It would cause beautiful, Retrogressive-stifling, liberty-protecting gridlock. Tea Party supporters don't want the government to "get something done" if that means enacting more laws and finding new and more devious ways to increase taxes (for example, by increasing the money supply).

The only thing they want politicians to do is repeal all unconstitutional legislation already on the books, get out of the way of the Entrepreneur and the private sector, and focus on protecting the lives and property of *all* U.S. citizens. Whether a citizen happens to be "rich" or "poor" is irrelevant—and, quite frankly, none of the government's business. While the concern of some politicians for the perceived hardship of any particular group of people may make for an interesting sociological or philosophical discussion, it does not give them the right to forcibly redistribute the assets of others.

Ignoring the Constitution

When I was a teenager, I recall asking in civics class, "What's to stop the president or Congress from ignoring the Constitution and doing whatever they please?" Predictably, the class laughed and the teacher patronizingly explained to me that our system of "checks and balances" made such a scenario impossible. I was too intimidated to press the matter further, but I do remember that I was totally unconvinced by my teacher's dismissive answer.

Now, after decades of increasing criminality in all three branches of government, I think it's safe to say that I've been vindicated. Presidents, Congresses, and the Supreme Court have been ignoring the Constitution—some even laughing about its irrelevance—for more than a hundred years, though most Americans have been oblivious to it. And when Retrogressives took control of the executive branch and both houses of Congress in 2009, they took it to another level and began thumbing their noses at their one-time employer—the people.

But didn't Barack Obama and all members of the House and Senate swear to uphold the Constitution? Sure, and when Adolf Hitler was legitimately chosen to be the chancellor of Germany in 1933 by President Paul von Hindenburg, he dutifully repeated the German oath of office at his swearing in ceremony: "I will employ my strength for the welfare of the German people, protect the Constitution and laws of the German people, conscientiously discharge the duties imposed on me, and conduct my affairs of office impartially and with justice to everyone."

Then, once in office, he moved swiftly and, within just a few weeks, established a dictatorship, a feat one might have thought would be impossible in a civilized Western democracy like Germany. But Hitler was an eloquent speaker who spoke incessantly about change. (Sound familiar?)

Big business supported Hitler, because the captains of industry felt certain that his policies would wreck the economy and thus lead to a return to authoritarian rule (which major corporations love, because it makes it easier for them to establish monopolies). What they did not count on, however, was that Hitler himself would be the one to grab the reins of power.

The upstart Nazi Party (which was the commonly used name for the National Socialist German Workers' Party . . . repeat, National *Socialist* German Workers' Party) staged a slobbering love affair between Hitler and the German people. (Sound familiar?) When Hitler spoke for the first time as chancellor, it was said that "he was greeted with an outpouring of worshipful adulation unlike anything ever seen before in Germany." (Sound familiar?)

In *The Road to Serfdom*, F. A. Hayek explains how countries travel the road leading from democracy to dictatorship:

Hitler did not have to destroy democracy; he merely took advantage of the decay of democracy and at the critical moment obtained the support of many to whom, though they detested Hitler, he yet seemed the only man strong enough to get things done.[4]

So if you're wondering how Obama and his Retrogressive cronies have been able to violate the Constitution as though it didn't exist, the answer is that they are merely taking advantage of the decay of democracy in the United States that was *already present* when they came to power. While Americans were busy watching *Desperate Housewives, The Bachelor,* and *The Apprentice,* the Retrogressive fascists in Washington were quietly working to establish a dictatorship.

Under the Articles of Confederation, the central government of America was very weak, which was a good thing. It was true then, and it is true now: You can have a strong government and a weak people, or a strong people and a weak government, but you cannot have both. Today, we have a draconian, out-of-control government and a very weak people.

Arguably, we began losing much of our freedom in this country as early as 1787, when the Constitution created a strong federal government. It got worse—much worse—under the fascist policies of Woodrow Wilson's reign from 1913 to 1921. Then, beginning in 1933, FDR's failed Retrogressive policies took even more individual liberty from American citizens, and the subsequent left-wing revolutionaries of the sixties set the stage for the final disintegration of liberty in this country.

Now, given Barack Obama's disastrous first term in office, what are the odds that he will be given four more years to finish his fundamental transformation of America? Well, after making the Great Depression even worse, FDR was re-elected anyway. And after four more years of the Great Depression, he was re-elected for an unprecedented third term . . . then, finally, a fourth!

When FDR mercifully croaked in 1945, he left, as his legacy to the nation, a fraudulent, anticonstitutional Social Security program, an antiprosperity tax structure, and a solid foundation for an entrenched welfare state that would grow out of control each year until it finally began to collapse early in the next century.

I remind you of all this to warn you that Barack Obama could conceivably be re-elected by a coalition of true-believing socialists, professional freeloaders, government workers, union members, and false-prosperity addicts.

That the government does not possess the right to spend your money against your will is morally self-evident, and it certainly is clear that it is unconstitutional. Yet, those on the left denigrate anyone who opposes them in their illegal pursuits by calling them "uncompassionate," "obstructionists," and "radicals." And it works!

But, morals aside (which is the way Retrogressives like to play the game), the fact is that government spending does *not* stimulate the economy. On the contrary, whether the government taxes, borrows, or prints to pay for its nefarious programs, its actions always have a negative impact on the economy. Only spending by individuals and companies can stimulate the economy, and the driving force behind that is *entrepreneurial activity*.

Unfortunately, "government by the people" has come to mean government by those in power. That's why, at the same time that unemployment in the private sector has risen dramatically, government jobs have actually *increased*—and government jobs do not stimulate the economy. The most powerful stimulus we need from Washington right now is for the government to cease all activities except for those spelled out in the Constitution. If there were no bailouts, no new spending, no new regulations, if government would just get out of the way of the Entrepreneur and stick to the job that we, the people, hired it to do—protect our lives and property—the economy would explode overnight.

Government, of course, is *not* going to get out of the way voluntarily. In the end, there are always plenty of shameless Republicans who end up capitulating. They make it sound as though they got big concessions from the Democrats in exchange for whatever compromise they agreed to, but the final outcome is always a political rape of Mr. and Mrs. America. Debates over cutting spending, raising the debt ceiling, and balancing the budget are nothing more than political theater for the masses.

The reason the Republican Party is on the verge of extinction is that, in the end, a majority of Republicans always give in to the intimidation tactics of the left when they are admonished to "reach across the aisle" and "compromise." The problem with reaching across the aisle is that the reaching is, for the most part, one-way—from right to left.

Compromise sounds like a noble goal until you examine it closely. How do you compromise between constitutional and unconstitutional? Between moral and immoral? Between responsible and irresponsible? Between freedom and slavery? In the real world of politics, compromise is but a euphemism for liberalism, liberalism is a euphemism for retrogressivism, retrogressivism is a euphemism for Marxism, Marxism is a euphemism for communism, and communism is a euphemism for totalitarian rule.

And by ignoring the Constitution, that is precisely what the Retrogressive fascists in D.C. are after—totalitarian rule. Never—ever—delude yourself on this point! Naiveté is an invitation to servitude.

The Extinction of Our Moral Foundation

When I started writing about America's decline more than three decades ago, it was my contention that it was not collapsing, per se. Rather, the America of our Founding Fathers was simply fading into the sunset of history through a phenomenon known as "gradualism," while Americans were watching *Monday Night Football*, guzzling Bud Light, and stuffing themselves with Big Macs.

They simply ignored the whole situation, because to comprehend it would have required not only thinking, but the courage to face truth squarely in the eye. And, unfortunately, most people fear truth, especially when it threatens to interfere with their false prosperity.

In twenty-first-century America, we are witnessing the long-awaited triumph of Rousseau's relativism. Certitudes are out; slavishness—in dress, eating, thinking, and speaking—is in. These are the underpinnings of our slide toward collectivism and an anything-goes society where people demand that their desires be fulfilled, without regard to the natural rights of others.

What made the United States unique for nearly two hundred years was that it generated the moral oxygen of dignity, civility, and ethics needed to keep the Western soul of the human race breathing. Americans actually had a sense of right and wrong. Not theoretical right and wrong, but absolute right and wrong based on certitudes.

Our certitudes weren't handed down to us on stone tablets (although the certitudes on the stone tablets did, for the most part, form the foundation for our own certitudes). The certitudes of Western culture were based on a "generally accepted code of conduct" that was pretty much in line with what has long been referred to as *Judeo-Christian values.*

In the United States, that was a pretty simple proposition. Since most Americans were Christians, Jews, or rational, civilized atheists (as opposed to hateful, disparaging atheists), there was an unspoken consensus. Maybe life wasn't fair by some people's standards, but it wasn't confusing, either. Everyone understood the rules. Then along came the hippies in the sixties, preaching the religion of relativism. Nothing, they insisted, is certain; everything is relative.

Worst of all, the government became involved in education, which was an important step in ridding us of those old-fashioned certitudes. Did you know that high-school history texts now devote considerable space to such American paragons of virtue as H. Rap Brown, Stokely

Carmichael, and Timothy Leary? "Turn on, tune in, drop out" is now right up there with General Sherman's "War is hell." As one certitude after another has been shouted out of existence by radical, boisterous Retrogressives, it has become an open invitation for people devoid of morals to push the envelope of decadence ever closer to the edge.

All this may cause some anarchists to cheer, but there's one problem they haven't considered. Out-of-control violence is a natural offspring of an anything-goes society, a society in which all certitudes have been quashed. And that's when a nation becomes a dictatorship waiting to happen. Retrogressives like to refer to it as "top down, bottom up"—foment "civil unrest" among the masses, then use it as an excuse to crack skulls and establish an authoritarian government.

Junk TV, gambling resorts to accommodate people who can barely afford to put food on their tables, abortions on demand, the acceptance of one-parent families as the norm, pretending that rap is poetry and/or music and that paint splashed on a canvas is "art," advertisements that appeal to society's lowest common denominator—collectively, these seemingly disparate phenomena have helped poison American minds and lay the groundwork for a collective entitlement mind-set.

Today, there is no such thing as absolute right and wrong. There is only fun . . . fun that everyone is entitled to . . . delirious, mind-numbing, nonstop fun. And none of this is by accident. Professional politicians know that anything that will keep the minds of the masses occupied with frivolity helps to shield them from the truth. Keep them laughing, keep them excited, keep them thinking fun at all times. The Oprah Slumber is the opium of today's masses.

Muddling Through

I am often asked if I believe that a "soft landing" for the U.S. economy might still be possible. I guess the answer to that question depends upon how you define *soft landing*. If by *soft landing* you mean that we will somehow muddle through, things will calm down on their own, and we will be able to avoid experiencing a great deal of pain, the answer is no. But if your definition of *soft landing* is an economy that declines one step at a time, without a great deal of anarchy and violence, I would say that such a scenario is possible. It all depends on how fast the government pushes the socialist envelope.

For decades the United States seems to have found a way to muddle through in spite of its political and fiscal indiscretions, which has led many to believe that we will continue to find ways to survive despite the fact that we are bankrupt, overregulated, and overtaxed, and that our corrupt and criminal rulers flout their total disregard for the Constitution they swore to uphold when they took office. Times may get terrible, inflation may destroy our currency, unemployment may reach 20 percent, but, in the end, America's superiority as a nation will prevail and preserve our way of life. Or so the theory goes.

The problem with the idea of muddling through is that it ignores the mountain of civilization-destroying realities that are already firmly entrenched in our society. To be sure, life will go on if we muddle through, but not necessarily in the manner to which you and I have become accustomed. That has become increasingly evident since Retrogressives took control of the White House and both houses of Congress in 2009, though they did lose some traction after the 2010 elections when the House gained eighty-seven new members who were mostly proentrepreneur and anti–big government.

Human beings have an uncanny ability to get used to bad circumstances and become immune to pain. Thus, my concern is that if we return to a more gradual collapse of our economy (i.e., a pre-Obama collapse), Americans will get used to a step-by-step lower standard of living, the result being that they will come to think of each new level as normal. Every new bailout, every new regulation, every new tax will cause a downward shift in the economy. That's not really muddling *through*; it's muddling *downward*—in stages—and giving people a chance to catch their collective breath and adapt to the next lower level.

Gradualism has worked like magic for the U.S. government for at least a hundred years, and it could once again protect politicians against outright rebellion. Norman Thomas, six-time presidential candidate for the Socialist Party of America, clearly understood the power of gradualism when he prophesied, "The American people will never knowingly adopt socialism, but under the name of liberalism they will adopt every fragment of the socialist program until one day America will be a socialist nation without ever knowing how it happened."

The average American has been adjusting to a gradual shift toward socialism for decades, because soft socialism made it possible for him to buy a house he couldn't afford, go on vacations he couldn't afford, and fill his life with hi-tech toys he couldn't afford. This comfy lifestyle made him oblivious to the fact that it was all a financial house of cards.

So long as our slide into socialism was gradual, people adapted to it. But as a result of Obama's lightning-fast moves, what we've experienced over the past several years has been a quick and major *visible* drop in living standards, which has made folks quite angry. So, with the 2012 elections looming on the horizon, Retrogressives realize they must move swiftly to achieve hard socialism, knowing that the Tea Party revolution will only become stronger. (It's pretty much shaping up as a race to the finish line between liberty and tyranny.)

More and more stopgap measures must be implemented in order to prevent thousands of government giveaway programs from collapsing. Unfortunately, though millions have now awakened from their false-prosperity slumber, there are just as many people who are still in a trance, still believing that redistribution of wealth is a good thing and that they will somehow get the better of the swindle.

I should mention here that there are those who believe

we will be able to continue muddling through because of scientific and technological advances so vast in scope that the Entrepreneur will soon be able to fulfill the desires of even the most GAVEAD-prone nonproducers. Ultimately, so the theory goes, there will be such an abundance of food, housing, medicines, and even the luxuries of life that they can be made available to the ever-growing army of entitlement folks.

I have the utmost faith in science and technology, but human nature dampens my optimism. It is highly doubtful that nonproducers will ever be satisfied, regardless of how many inexpensive (or free) goods and services they receive as a result of advances in technology. As we have witnessed with public-sector union uprisings from coast to coast, free stuff merely whets the appetite of society's parasites for unlimited wealth without work.

The Party of *No*

Retrogressives have grown fond of labeling Republicans "the party of no," which causes many GOP establishment types to fall all over themselves trying to assure the public that they sincerely want to work with their "colleagues" across the aisle. Big mistake. Rather than fearing the label, Republicans should embrace it. If the Republican Party intends to get back to its pro-Constitution, free-market, small-government, reduced-spending roots, it should be proud to be called the party of *no*.

After Barack Obama's first year in the White House, he claimed that his only failure was that he had not been good enough at getting his message across. On the contrary, he was so good at getting his message across that a majority of voters clearly understood that he did, indeed, want to fundamentally transform America into a collectivist society.

The people who have to do better at getting their message across are the Republicans. They should have the courage to say boldly and unequivocally, "We *are* the party of *no,* and we're proud of it. No to socialized medicine; no to more bailouts; no to government taking over private companies; no to radicals being appointed to high positions in government by the president; no to government involvement in the Internet; no to more government spending; no to raising the debt ceiling; no to government snooping on private citizens; no, no, no."

And, of course, no to Obamacare. But in saying no to Obamacare, Republicans do not need to come up with another version of "healthcare reform." What they need to do is insist that the government get *completely* out of the healthcare business, and they can start that process by repealing Obamacare and proposing that all regulations preventing the purchase of healthcare across state lines be abolished. Most Americans don't want more laws. What they want is for most of the laws already on the books to be *repealed.*

Since Obama's favorability rating is still around 45 percent (at the time of the writing of this book), one has to assume that those who are still giving him a thumbs-up are either totally uninformed or hard-core socialists (or worse). My guess is that the latter group comprises somewhere between 25 and 30 percent of the population. Admittedly, that's a rather depressing figure, but, thankfully, it's still a minority.

The good news is that all hell is breaking loose around the media-perpetrated lie known as "Barack Hussein Obama": so-called stimulus bills that succeed only in stimulating unemployment, terrorists being Mirandaized and afforded the same rights as U.S. citizens, an in-your-face determination to foist some form of government-controlled healthcare and cap-and-trade legislation on the American people against their will, record budget deficits, with no end in sight, nonstop threats and ridicule aimed at detractors, and on and on the list goes.

Far-left radicals have made it clear, since at least the days of Vladimir Lenin, that anything—including, and especially, lying—is justified in the pursuit of ends they deem to be morally desirable. Which is why I have long been concerned about the occurrence of a sudden event that could be used to justify a phony state of emergency to head off an election in 2012 if it becomes clear that Democrats are going to suffer an even greater defeat than they did in 2010.

There's no way to predict what such an event might be, because the possibilities are endless. Remember, the government used a hurricane—Katrina—to justify taking guns away from law-abiding citizens. What the hell does a hurricane have to do with a law-abiding citizen owning a gun, other than the fact that his need to protect himself and his family is *greater* if thugs are roaming the streets, looting and pillaging?

To the delight of the hard left, the fork-in-the-road debate continues in the Republican Party to this day: "Shall we be inclusive and bring more Retrogressives into the party, or shall we remain steadfast to traditional conservative principles?" In *Liberty and Tyranny*, Mark Levin quotes Michael Gerson, former chief speechwriter for George W. Bush, from his book *Heroic Conservatism*: "If Republicans run in future elections with a simplistic anti-government message, ignoring the poor, the addicted and children at risk, they will lose, and they will deserve to lose."

As the 2010 elections demonstrated, Gerson had it 180 degrees wrong. On the contrary, I believe small-government Republicans should invite the Retrogressives in their own party to become Democrats. Republicans need to clear their tent (the departures of Arlen Specter and Charlie "The Hug" Crist were a good start in that direction) in order to make room for the next wave of Tea Party congressmen.

If Republicans want to put the final nail in their extinction coffin, they need only continue making compromise their badge of honor. Many party members believe that the way to power (which, unfortunately, is what politics is all about) is for them to be better bone throwers than the

Democrats—i.e., to throw more bones to "the poor," to the unemployed, to "minorities," to union members, to the elderly, to those whose houses are in foreclosure, and just about anyone else who claims to be in need. The problem is that every bone that is thrown only succeeds in bringing cries for still more bones, until, alas, there are no more tax-payer bones to throw. And *that* is when America is going to hit the wall with financial shock and awe the likes of which the world has never before witnessed.

Free political advice to incumbent Republicans: If you want to get re-elected in 2012, forget the "adult conversation" babble that Republican leadership is promoting and listen to what the Tea Party people are saying. And what they're saying is: No! Your willingness to do so will go a long way toward determining whether it is too late for America to return to its founding principles.

8.

THE PERPETUAL, TITANIC STRUGGLE

In an article in the *New York Times* titled "Who Will Tell the People?" Thomas Friedman, not exactly a conservative, wrote: "We don't need a president who is tough enough to withstand the lies of his opponents. We need a president who is tough enough to tell the truth to the American people." Friedman went on to say, "We are not who we think we are. We are living on borrowed time and borrowed dimes. We still have all the potential for greatness, but only if we get back to work on our country." [1]

So, who will tell the people the truth? So far, no one, because politicians have convinced themselves that they can't get elected by being too truthful. That's because most people do not love truth; instead, they try to make true that which they love. For example, all candidates are well aware of the fact that there is no constituency for cutting entitlements, so they know they have only two choices: lie or lose.

Unfortunately, recognizing that power has such a corrupting influence on those who achieve it, many honorable individuals refuse to run for office. The very nature of a republic, or, even worse, a democracy, makes it virtually impossible for a politician to adhere to the principles of true liberty and still manage to keep getting elected. I believe that some people come to Washington with sincere intentions to roll back big government, eliminate federal handout programs, and abolish antifreedom laws and regulations. But once in power, they become convinced of the need to buy votes, lest they find themselves out of the club and having to—gasp!—seek employment in the private sector.

Nevertheless, as a result of the Tea Party phenomenon, perhaps as many as 60 percent of Americans are finally ready to hear the truth. Regrettably, a majority of the remaining 40 percent or so will *never* be ready. They will always be stuck on demanding and getting whatever they want, regardless of whether it violates someone else's rights and regardless of whether taxpayers can afford to give it to them.

There is no question that it takes a great deal of courage and integrity for a politician to share the harsh economic facts of life with the public. It means that Republicans would have to do a one-eighty from their decades of trying to mimic and outbid Democrats in an effort to gain votes. It means they would have to summon up the toughness to tell their constituents—straightforwardly and without qualification—that they must be willing to accept a great deal of hardship, even suffering, if they have a sincere desire to save their children and grandchildren not only from poverty, but from servitude as well.

The foundation for this dilemma was laid by FDR some eighty years ago. Once hundreds of New Deal and Great Society programs were put into place, Democrats and Republicans rarely spoke about cutting the budget, and anyone who suggested such a far-out idea was viewed as an extremist. This clever "new-baseline" strategy is the key to retrogressivism: Get a bill passed (e.g., healthcare), establish a baseline, then, in the future, debate is restricted only to what the percentage of *increase* should be each year for that particular chunk of the budget.

Thus, current levels of expenditures always become the new baseline. Retrogressives know all too well that once a program is on the books, no one will have the temerity to suggest completely removing it. And, of course, anyone who challenges the new-baseline strategy is vilified as cruel and callous, a psychological ploy Retrogressives have been using since our experiment in soft socialism began. So, instead, both sides continually babble about such abstracts as "reforming entitlements" and "cutting waste, fraud, and abuse," always being careful to stay away from specifics.

If our republic is to be saved from its own democratic excesses, our only hope is for a libertarian-centered conservative presidential candidate to step up to the plate and, with exceptional honesty and courage, tell people the truth—that neither the government nor anyone else has a right to anything they earn or own, and that they, in turn, do not have a right to anything that anyone else earns or owns. They must be told that it's fine to love your neighbor, but that no one has a right to force you to take care of his medical needs, or support him if he loses his job, or hire him at a wage politicians deem to be fair, or provide aid to him in any other way.

From octomoms in California to welfare bums in Massachusetts, from environmentalists in Oregon to heroin addicts in New York City, no one has a right to force anyone else to accommodate his desires just because he refers to them as *needs*. And by no stretch of the imagination can anyone's "needs" be transformed into rights. The only rights an individual possesses are those given to him by God at birth.

What is needed is a presidential candidate who will make it clear that it is time for the federal government to obey the Constitution. Which means having the backbone to say, without apology, such things as:

- "If elected, I will do everything in my power to first reduce, then completely phase out, *all* welfare programs. This includes unemployment benefits, food stamps, and all other transfer-of-wealth schemes."

- "If elected, I will do everything in my power to eliminate the minimum wage, which creates unemployment and ravages the economy."

- "If elected, I will do everything in my power to get the government completely out of the economy and eliminate draconian government regulations."

- "If elected, I will do everything in my power to limit federal authority and return sovereignty to the individual states."

- "If elected, I will do everything in my power to cut off *all* federal funding for abortions."

- "If elected, I will do everything in my power to phase out Social Security and allow people to keep, save, and invest their own money as they see fit. This would be done over a long period of time, so people who have been counting on Social Security in their old age would not be hurt."

- "If elected, I will do everything in my power to repeal Obamacare."

Further, he must explain to the people that, among other things:

- The government has no constitutional or moral authority to be involved in banking.

- The government has no constitutional or moral authority to be involved in the automobile business.

- The government has no constitutional or moral authority to be involved in education.

- The government has no constitutional or moral authority to be involved in funding "community organizers"—or any other groups—whether they do or don't promote prostitution, tax evasion, or election fraud.

- And the government certainly has no constitutional or moral authority to be involved in redistributing wealth.

The Efficacy of a Deflationary Depression

But perhaps the toughest thing of all for this ideal presidential candidate to explain to voters is why a deflationary depression would be a good thing for them—and all of America—over the long term.

The reason it would be so difficult to convince voters that a deflationary depression is the quickest and best solution for America's financial ills is that, in contrast to the slow downward shift in living standards that results from gradualism, a quick and total deflationary collapse would bring about sharp pain. And the reason for this is that, unlike 1929 and the onset of the Great Depression, today a large percentage of the population has a deeply ingrained entitlement mind-set. Thus, few people are interested in hearing that the best solution to America's financial ills is to face the consequences of our financial indiscretions now rather than later.

So I ask you: Are you prepared to lower your standard of living—even suffer—so your children and grandchildren can enjoy a better standard of living than you? An even more important question may be: Are you prepared to lower your standard of living to stave off the possibility that your children and grandchildren might live under totalitarian rule? Finally, the moral question: Are you prepared to face the constitutional reality that you are entitled to absolutely nothing other than the right to pursue your own success and happiness in any way you choose, so long as you do not violate the natural rights of others in the process?

Bluntly speaking, are you prepared to go "cold turkey"— to give up (a false sense of) security in exchange for freedom? I'm sorry to say that my personal take on the pulse of our country is that not many people are. Which is why few politicians are willing to name *specific* government entitlements they would eliminate. (Not cut—*eliminate.*)

It's a constitutional fact that it is not the government's duty (or right) to support people who have lost their jobs, retrain them for a different profession, or save them from losing their homes. Sorry, but job loss and job retraining, along with losing one's home through foreclosure, while worthy and interesting subjects to ponder and discuss, are not covered in the Constitution.

Some economists, in what seems like a desperate attempt to justify government interference in the marketplace, argue that false prosperity is better than risking a depression. (The polite phrase is "severe recession.") They could not be more wrong. As I have pointed out so often, the truth is that we've been in an *invisible* depression for at least thirty years. We are in dire need of a deflationary depression, because it is a natural adjustment period in the supply-and-demand cycle that forces people and businesses to become more efficient.

It's a "reprimand" for being naughty—for people treating themselves to the fantasy that prosperity can be created without work. The more irresponsible their actions, the worse the reprimand. Just as it is in the long-term best interest of children to be taught a lesson by getting an occasional spanking for misbehaving, so it is with adults who have been financially irresponsible.

Does this mean I lack compassion? No. On the contrary, I have a great deal of compassion for the millions of people who are suffering financially. And, quite frankly, it makes me angry when I think about the fact that the main cause of their pain and suffering is the self-serving, anti-constitutional actions of politicians.

Above all, contrary to what politicians, the media, and most Americans seem to believe, it's not the government's job to "get the economy moving again." One more time: It's not in the Constitution! Economic stability can come about only by unleashing the creative genius of the Entrepreneur, allowing the market to take its natural course, and *ridding the economy of artificially created wealth.*

Long term, a deflationary depression would be a financial catharsis for Americans because people would be forced to live within their means. As a result, the price of just about every type of merchandise would fall to a level where it could be sold, overvalued investments would drop to realistic plateaus, and, when everything reached its natural level once more, the market would again be healthy. Which is why, if it's important to you that your progeny live better than you're living today, you should hope that things unravel quickly.

Unfortunately, even when faced with imminent financial disaster as a result of the economic maelstrom they have created, our Retrogressive politicians are not likely to fess up. Instead, hiding behind the Federal Reserve, they will go for the easiest escape route—inflation—because they are convinced that people will never willingly accept a lower standard of living. As even the most hard-core Retrogressive understands, both taxing the rich and borrowing have their limitations. But printing more fiat currency requires only that the government be able to purchase paper and ink—and pay its electric bill.

And the nice thing about inflation of the money supply is that it's an *invisible* tax. As prices rise, people cannot keep pace, and their standard of living drops. But they don't know why. Thus, the government can point its soiled finger at "corporate greed," "the rich," special-interest groups— same old class-warfare act.

Wanted: A Courageous Capitalist

Instead of pinning our hopes on a courageous and honest politician with the courage to tell the truth, perhaps we'd have better luck with a high-profile capitalist who would be willing to step front and center and defend capitalism and entrepreneurship as the essential ingredients in creating a healthy economy and higher standard of living for everyone who is willing to work. One would think that those who have become wealthy through the capitalist system would be the first to defend it, but I hearken back to the words of Henry Ford II, who said, in a speech at the University of Chicago Business School Management Conference in 1979:

The market, which has rendered American capitalism more humane and effective, is the very thing which the enemies of capitalism have traditionally distrusted the most. But because of our shortcomings we have not been able to make a very strong case for the market.

I sometimes suspect that many American capitalists actually distrust the market as much as capitalism's enemies do. There are whole industries today that prefer to escape the market's disciplines.

Such businessmen only encourage those who seek reform through the government, who seek greater regulation of business and greater governmental control over the private sector. But solutions like those are alien to our national experience, and American capitalism has a duty to fight them.

That we have failed to hold up our end of this fight is clear. But it is not too late for us to mend our ways. We have not gone so far down the road of government intervention that we cannot turn back.²

The Perpetual, Titanic Struggle

Henry Ford II died in 1987, and since his death, capitalists, unfortunately, have not turned back. On the contrary, today, more than ever, too many capitalists fight for government intervention on their behalf. Sadly, capitalists are often the worst enemies of laissez-faire capitalism and the justice of the market.

Nothing is more self-defeating than hypocrisy. Capitalism is not something to be defensive about; it's a system to be proud of. Aside from the moral superiority of capitalism, a nice bonus is that economic freedom gives those at the bottom of the economic ladder the greatest opportunity to better their existence through entrepreneurship—and, in the process, create jobs and grow the economy.

The great individualist and free-market champion Frank Chodorov put it squarely on the line when he wrote:

If, for instance, those who prate about "free enterprise" were willing to risk bankruptcy for it, even as the men of the Declaration risked their necks for independence (their lives, their fortunes, and their sacred honor), the present drive for the collectivization of capital would not have such easy going. Assuming that they are fully aware of the implications of the phrase they mouth, and are sincere in their protestations, the fact that they are unwilling to suffer mortification of the flesh disqualifies them for leadership, and the case for "free enterprise" is hopeless.[3]

In simple terms, what Chodorov was saying was that if capitalists are unwilling to put their time and money where their mouths are, then the case for freedom and free enterprise will be lost by default. Chodorov, who passed away in 1966, would have had great scorn for men like Warren Buffett, Ted Turner, and Bill Gates. All of them have been charitable, which is admirable, but I would argue that had these men focused their time and energies on preaching the gospel of capitalism and entrepreneurship to the masses, they would have accomplished far more for the poorest among us over the long term.

Take Gates, for example. Having taken his obligatory place in history as a great philanthropist, he follows in the footsteps of such legendary capitalists/Entrepreneurs as Andrew Carnegie, John D. Rockefeller, and Henry Ford. To be sure, a $29 billion foundation dedicated to fighting, among other things, Third-World disease and poverty is a noble undertaking. Still, you can feed people, vaccinate them, and provide them with shelter only until your money runs out. Even if every dime of Gates's $29 billion foundation reached the needy in Africa, it wouldn't do much good over the long term. The reality is that $29 billion is a drop in the bucket when it comes to providing millions of people with food, shelter, medical care, and education. So, from a long-term point of view, it's all in vain if you don't address the underlying causes of disease and poverty.

And the biggest cause by far is, and always has been, brutal, corrupt, dictatorial governments that suppress and terrorize their own citizens and make entrepreneurship all but impossible. The only thing that can permanently solve the problem of widespread poverty is freedom—which, by definition, includes free markets. Haitians do not need charity (which seemed not to help them at all) as much as they need freedom. When market forces are unleashed and people are free to pursue their own well-being, entrepreneurship flourishes and everyone's standard of living rises.

I guess I'm neither vain enough nor smart enough to come up with a solution for Third World countries ruled by serial killers. But if Gates really wants to help impoverished people, he should devote his efforts to making the civilized world more prosperous and hope that much of the increased wealth would find its way to Third World countries via U.S overseas ventures (as it has in India, for example), which in turn would lead to foreign entrepreneurial activity and its natural offspring, economic growth.

How could Gates accomplish this? By doling out his foundation's entire $29 billion in interest-free loans to Western Entrepreneurs, particularly Entrepreneurs who are down and out and have no collateral to back their loans. I'm talking about the millions of men and women who have had the courage to put it all on the line and ended up losing everything. These heroes are potential wealth-builders who are champing at the bit for another chance to prove themselves.

A nice dream, to be sure, but I have a suspicion that Bill Gates is not in the market for my advice.

The sad reality is that we can't count on billionaires to save America any more than we can count on politicians. Each of us has to do our part to help our fellow citizens rediscover the morals, ethics, and values that once served as the foundation of American superiority. Smart Entrepreneurs clearly understand how the invisible hand of the marketplace works, even though most Americans have no clue. Economic freedom is the best friend of those who are most impoverished—and it's a friendship governments hate.

Will Atlas Shrug?

In Greek mythology, Atlas was the deity that carried the entire world on his broad shoulders. So it's not surprising that Ayn Rand, in her novel *Atlas Shrugged*, used Atlas as a metaphor for the Entrepreneur. That's right, every Entrepreneur is an Atlas—and if the Entrepreneur ever decides to throw in the towel (i.e., shrug), it will surely ring down the final curtain on America's grand experiment in freedom.

In the case of the Founding Fathers, it was more than just a shrug. After being oppressed by their government for decades, they reluctantly put their lives, their fortunes, and their sacred honor on the line and resorted to violence to win their freedom. They made their feelings about it clear in the Declaration of Independence when they said:

The Perpetual, Titanic Struggle

But when a long train of abuses and usurpations, pursuing invariably the same Object evinces a design to reduce them under absolute Despotism, it is their right, it is their duty, to throw off such Government, and to provide new Guards for their future security.

But that was then, and this is now. Today, the one thing of which you can be certain is that producers will be taxed at ever-higher rates to appease the millions of GAVEAD-afflicted people who demand "social justice." Which makes you wonder, at what point will producers simply give up and stop producing?

Interestingly, in the past, most producers continued to create wealth even when their taxes rose to draconian levels. During World War II, for example, the top tax rate reached 94 percent, and it remained at 91 percent until 1964. However, I believe that was an anomalous period in our history. World War II was a very popular war, and we came out of that conflict a unified and patriotic nation. It wasn't until the mid-sixties that everything began to unravel, in no small part due to the very *un*popular war in Vietnam.

Nevertheless, even today I believe producers would continue producing for a reasonable period of time even if they had to share ever-larger slices of their pie with non-producers. I also believe that long before a level of total confiscation is reached (shades of Obama Sr.'s 100 percent income tax), producers would figure out what is happening, which would result in tax evasion, black markets, and a refusal to work.

In other words, at some point—and no one knows exactly when that might be—producers might just decide to pack it in and escape to Galt's Gulch. It may not be a physical place, as it was in *Atlas Shrugged*, but when it is no longer worth their effort, they will simply stop producing—and many will even expatriate.

Simply put, if the relentless march of retrogressivism is not halted, Atlas will, indeed, shrug. And that shrug will lead to the rather awkward problem of what to do when there is no more wealth available to redistribute. False-prosperity addicts have made it clear that they have no interest in hearing that the well has run dry. They still want it all, and they want it now.

Which is why, if Atlas does shrug, it should prove to be quite an interesting dilemma for the Retrogressive—a dilemma he can solve only by establishing an authoritarian government that would have the power to silence the discontent of those who continue to demand a return to their artificial good life.

The Liberty-Education Solution

For more than thirty years, I have maintained that the best way to contain the Retrogressive's relentless drive to destroy capitalism, entrepreneurship, and freedom is through a massive, grassroots, liberty-education program. When all is said and done, I believe it's up to you and me to carry the torch and educate others about the morality and efficacy of freedom and free markets. And in doing so, we should not allow ourselves to become sidetracked by oil spills, union riots, foiled terrorist plots, and other issues that take the focus off of our loss of liberty.

That means reading, learning, and spreading the word one person at a time. Start with your own children, who most probably are being, or have been, brainwashed by teachers and professors steeped in GAVEAD. Then talk to friends, coworkers, other family members, and anyone else who has an open mind. What's at stake? Everything. Because if the liberty-education revolution is not won, the revolution from the left—which believes in the use of violence to force its will on others—will surely prevail.

We were never intended to be a collectivist society. Our Founding Fathers fought for a society based on individual rights, entrepreneurship, and liberty for all. Government is the enemy not only of the Entrepreneur, but of all people of goodwill whose lives are enhanced by the Entrepreneur's efforts. Again, as Thomas Paine pointed out nearly 250 years ago, government, even in its best state, is but a necessary evil.

Since the true cause of the disintegration of American culture was a revolution of moral relativism, I believe its rebirth can be brought about only through another moral revolution—a revolution that rejects the notion that a person has a right to anything he desires. And the fact is that morals are not inherited; they are learned.

Thus, to rediscover the morals, ethics, and values that once served as the foundation of Western civilization, the majority of people in our society must be re-educated. They must be taught to reject the belief that it is moral to violate the rights of others simply by outvoting them. Which means they must learn to challenge the premise that anything a majority decides is moral by default. Tyranny of the majority is *immoral.*

People must be taught that no matter how compassionate a person may believe his cause to be, it does not give him the right to use force against others to achieve his ends. On the contrary, they must be taught that individual sovereignty is the most sacred right of every human being. Above all, they must be taught that clinging to their government-created artificial good life comes at the cost of their freedom, as well as the freedom of future generations.

The Retrogressive insists that anyone who is against government handouts lacks compassion. But what's compassionate about a professional politician taking *your* money by force and giving it to someone of *his* choice? The most compassionate people I know are strictly opposed to the use of force (including the use of force for the purported purpose of helping the "truly needy"). The essence of a liberty-education revolution would be to teach people that only *voluntary* compassion is moral, that compulsory compassion is coercion, and that coercion is *always* immoral. In truth, political compassion is about nothing more than seizing and maintaining power by buying off voters.

If mass education on the subject of morality is to succeed, high-profile libertarians and conservatives must have the courage to tell Americans, clearly and boldly: "You, my friends, are entitled to nothing. You are not entitled to a car; you are not entitled to a job; you are not entitled to healthcare; you are not entitled to a roof over your head; you are not even entitled to one square meal a day. What you are entitled to is exactly what you can earn in a free market—meaning what others will voluntarily pay you for your services."

I say this not because I lack compassion, but because I believe that the sovereignty of the individual is supreme. Individual sovereignty and compassion are not mutually exclusive objectives. The Retrogressive has quite cleverly tried to tie the two together, but they are, in fact, unrelated. I believe in individual sovereignty, but I also consider myself to be a compassionate person. That's why I believe so strongly in private charity.

If we are to steer the USS *Titanic* away from the gigantic financial iceberg that lies just ahead, the entire concept of entitlements—*of any and all kinds*—must be rejected by a majority of Americans. The notion that anyone has a right to anything other than what others are willing to pay him, free of coercion, is Retrogressive nonsense. Those who place a higher value on liberty than all other objectives must not allow themselves to fall into the Retrogressive's false-compassion trap.

This will not be easy. For decades, Retrogressives have given teeth to the collectivist revolution by translating their immoral objectives into law. In addition, they have succeeded in convincing a majority of Americans that something is moral just because it is "legal"—continually admonishing them to be "law-abiding" citizens. The result is that plunder has long been accepted as moral simply because it is officially decreed and sanctioned by law. And if one refuses to conform, he does so at the risk of being ostracized by friends and associates—or, worse, ending up in jail.

While the needs and desires of certain individuals may be a legitimate concern for many people, they nonetheless fall outside the scope of man's natural rights. This does not mean that a person should not be concerned about others. It does not mean that a person should not be sympathetic toward others. It does not mean that a person should not be helpful to others. And it does not mean that a person should not be charitable to others.

What it does mean is that no person has a right to *force* others to be concerned, sympathetic, helpful, or charitable to others. As Frederic Bastiat put it, "The purpose of the law is not to be philanthropic; it is to protect people's property." How dare some arrogant politician tell you that he wants to spread *your* wealth around? Why doesn't he just spread his *own* wealth around? To paraphrase the late Milton Friedman, everyone has a right to help those he deems to be in need to whatever extent he desires—with his *own* money.

Decades of socialist brainwashing have made the task

ahead of us enormous. And the first step in that task is to understand that the only hope for a solution to the economic disaster Americans now face is to start asking the right questions. Because of the success of the Retrogressive's moral revolution, most political arguments are based on false premises that are now considered sacrosanct.

To turn things around in this country, people must be taught to let go of these false premises. It is the only way they can be intellectually free to ask the right questions.

For example, they need to be taught to ask:

- Not "Is majority rule best for the greatest number of people?" but "Is majority rule, as it is now practiced, moral at all?"

- Not "Does the present tax structure really help the people it is intended to help?" but "Is the present tax structure constitutional?"

- Not "Is enough effort being put forth to cut waste from federal programs?" but "Why do most federal programs even exist?"

- Not "What should the government do to solve people's problems?" but "Why should the government be involved in solving people's problems at all?"

Unfortunately, the reality is that millions of people want more benefits, not less. Worse, they have absolutely no understanding of the moral ramifications of their actions, and only recently have started to see the economic consequences of America's soft socialism policies of the past eighty years.

At the same time, their minds are being scrambled by a new wave of younger, slicker Retrogressives who are masters at appealing to the GAVEAD in voters and convincing them that greedy corporations, greedy Wall Streeters, and greedy rich folks are the chief cause of our financial ills.

"But," you may ask, "what's the use of becoming involved in a liberty-education program when you've already assured me that financial catastrophe for the United States is all but impossible to avoid?"

There is no question that Americans will have to experience much more pain and suffering before they will be ready to even consider listening to real solutions that are now looked upon as radical. What is not certain, however, is which radical solutions they will listen to. This will be the deciding factor when it comes to America's future, because one set of solutions will lead to an authoritarian government and a total loss of liberty, while the other will lead to freedom and prosperity. The reality is that the United States is now embroiled in a second civil war. The divide between liberty and tyranny is irreconcilable, and it's time for those who believe in liberty to come to grips with this reality.

The good guys have the numbers (roughly 70–30), but the bad guys have the loud voices, the willingness to resort to violence, and, currently, control of the military. Which means that our freedom may ultimately boil down to whether the military will be willing to move against American citizens when ordered to do so or whether it will, instead, turn on its masters.

The question is straightforward: Can we, as a people, rediscover the morals, ethics, and values that once served as the foundation of our once-great country? In my view, the only way we can hope to do that is by having the courage, the wisdom, and the insight to first acknowledge the realities. The reason solutions offered by politicians, academicians, and media pundits have proven to be useless is that they totally ignore the underlying moral problem that has been destroying America for decades.

It's strictly up to us. We can continue to be the United States of Stuff, or we can wake up, grow up, and push back *hard* against an oppressive government led by power-hungry Retrogressives. At the end of the day, it's a clear choice between submission and all-out resistance in an effort to re-establish the foundation of our once free and proud republic.

Once that foundation is restored, America's great unsung hero, the Entrepreneur, will be free to rise up and begin moving America's economic fortunes forward at mach speed. But, while doing so, he must keep one eye on the Retrogressive, who will forever be quietly plotting new and more clever ways to appeal to the GAVEAD instincts in people in the hope of fundamentally transforming America into a collectivist hell.

If we are to return to the roots of our founding, Retrogressive subjectivism must be resisted by whatever means necessary. Go-along-to-get-along conservatism does not work. To compromise on principles is to lie, and lies always bring bad endings. Most politicians don't get it, but the Tea Party people do.

The Retrogressive is, of course, free to believe whatever suits his intellectual and moral needs. But he must not be allowed to force others to give up their freedom to accommodate his twisted notion regarding one of the most subjective and abstract concepts known to man: "fairness"—a notion that has been even more abstractly relabeled "social justice." The only kind of fairness or social justice that makes any sense, certainly from a moral standpoint, is for everyone to keep what he earns in a free market.

Who Shall Prevail?

Thus, the major question of our time is, which side shall prevail? Will it be the Retrogressive, who extols the virtues of a collectivist society in which men and women are living, breathing automatons? Or will it be the rational, civilized, freedom-loving adult who passionately believes in the right of the individual to determine his own destiny, to work as hard as he chooses, to earn as much as he possibly can, and to keep the fruits of his labor?

It is the entrepreneurial spirit that has always moved

America forward, which is why I believe it is the Entrepreneur who is most capable of leading the charge to resurrect the American way of life that our parents and grandparents experienced. And if he can accomplish that gargantuan feat, he will rightly deserve to take his place alongside George Washington, Thomas Jefferson, and other giants of the American Revolution.

Set free to act in his own best interest, the Entrepreneur has the capacity to be the driving force behind a new and revitalized America with unlimited possibilities for improving the well-being of its citizens. By contrast, if, through a lack of vigilance on the part of those who believe in liberty, the Retrogressive is able to achieve the power to completely control our lives, he will likely bring about a new Dark Ages from which the world may never recover.

Keep in mind that the far left never retreats. It is patient. It has been trudging forward in America for at least a hundred years. Which is why the war between Retrogressive fascists and those who extol the virtues of liberty is never-ending. The cost of freedom is, indeed, eternal vigilance.

It is therefore important not to think in terms of overnight or outright victory in the war against tyranny. It won't happen. Not only is quick victory unachievable, total victory is not possible. The objective in this war must be containment, and that requires never-ending vigilance.

* * *

As Ronald Reagan said, "Freedom is never more than one generation away from extinction. We didn't pass it to our children in the bloodstream. It must be fought for, protected, and handed on for them to do the same."

The time has come for Americans to tell politicians that we don't want any more economic quick fixes. The only way for things to get better is for government to get out of the way and allow the Entrepreneur to move the country forward. It is the Entrepreneur, not government, who built America and made it the most prosperous country in the history of the world.

And he can do it again. All he needs is for the government to abide by the Constitution—to allow him to pursue his dreams without government interference, and with the freedom to create and compete on an equal footing with his counterparts in countries that reward, rather than punish, success—and America will once again become the last best hope of mankind.

Notes

Introduction

1. Ronald J. Pestritto and William J. Atto, *American Progressivism* (Lanham, MD: Lexington Books, 2008).
2. Will Durant, *The Greatest Minds and Ideas of All Time* (New York: Simon & Schuster, 2002).

1. The Entrepreneur as Hero

1. Paul J. Sarvadi, "Small Business Is the Backbone of America," *The Entrepreneurial Spirit,* http://www.allegrorealty.com/media/images/gallery/EntrepreneurialSpirit.pdf (Accessed May 19, 2011).

2. Putting It All on the Line

1. Baltasar Gracian (translated by Lawrence C. Lockley, Ph.D.), *Gracian's Science of Success and Art of Prudence* (San Jose: University of Santa Clara Press, 1967).

3. Whatever It Takes

1. James Wallace and Jim Erickson, *Hard Drive* (New York: John Wiley & Sons, 1992), 30.
2. Ibid., 163.

4. The Foundation for Entrepreneurship

1. Jeffrey Kluger, "Ambition: Why Some People Are Most Likely to Succeed," *Time*, November 9, 2005.
2. Barry Goldwater, *The Conscience of a Conservative* (New York: Victor Publishing Company, 1960).
3. Guy Murchie, *The Seven Mysteries of Life* (Boston: Houghton Mifflin Company, 1978).
4. "India Inc.," *Time*, June 26, 2006.
5. John Stossel, *Myths, Lies, and Downright Stupidity* (New York: Hyperion Books, 2006), 69–70.
6. Gustavo Arellano, "Congressman Darrell Issa to Oversee Federal Food Regulation: Good or Bad?" *OC Weekly,* January 11, 2011, http://blogs.ocweekly.com/stickaforkinit/2011/01/congressman_darrell_issa_to_ov.php.
7. "BE WORRIED. BE **VERY** WORRIED," *Time*, April 3, 2006.
8. Melanie Phillips, "The Global Warming Scam," January 9, 2004, http://www.freerepublic.com/focus/f-news/1055542/posts.

5. The Anti-entrepreneurial Holy Grail

1. Barack Obama, 2001 Chicago Public Radio interview, http://www.youtube.com/watch?v=OkpdNtTgQNM.
2. Ibid.

3. Ron Paul, *End the Fed* (New York: Grand Central Publishing, 2009).

4. Amity Shlaes, *The Forgotten Man* (New York: Harper Perennial, 2007, 2008).

5. William Graham Sumner, "The Forgotten Man and Other Essays," 1883, http://mises.org/books/forgottenman.pdf.

6. John C. Goodman, "What Is Classical Liberalism?" National Center for Policy Analysis, http://www.ncpa.org/pdfs/whatisclassicalliberalism.pdf (Accessed May 18, 2011).

7. Lyle H. Rossiter, Jr., M.D., *The Liberal Mind* (St. Charles, Ill.: Free World Books, 2006).

8. Donald Berwick, "Donald Berwick on Redistributing Wealth," http://www.youtube.com/watch?v=r2Kevz_9lsw.

9. Will Durant, *Caesar and Christ* (New York: Simon and Schuster, 1944).

10. Frederic Bastiat, *The Law* (New York: Tribeca Books, 2011), http://www.lexrex.com/informed/otherdocuments/thelaw/law03.htm.

11. Rossiter, *The Liberal Mind*,

12. Star Parker, "Parker and Keyes to Hold Conference," CURE, August 23, 2004, http://urbancure.org/print.asp?idarticle=3005.

6. The GAVEAD Syndrome

1. Ronald J. Pestritto and William J. Atto, *American Progressivism* (Lanham, Md.: Lexington Books, 2008).

2. Jesse Lee Peterson, *Scam* (Nashville: WND Books, 2003).

3. Frederick Douglass, "What shall we do with the Negro?" http://www.lexrex.com/enlightened/writings/douglas.htm (Accessed May 19, 2011).

4. Loren Eiseley, *The Immense Journey* (New York: Random House, 1959).

5. George Orwell, *Animal Farm* (New York: Harcourt, Brace, Jovanovich, 1946, 1974).

6. Alvin Toffler, *The Third Wave* (New York: William Morrow and Company, 1980).

7. Will and Ariel Durant, *The Lessons of History* (New York: Simon & Schuster, 2010), 72.

8. Sean Hannity interview of two University of Pittsburgh students at G-20 Summit in Pittsburgh, http://www .youtube.com/watch?v=vy3gxBuEFKY&playnext=1&list= PL1442C9DAEB62E28F (Accessed September 25, 2009).

9. Saul D. Alinsky, *Rules for Radicals* (New York: Random House, 1971).

10. Nathaniel Branden, *Judgment Day: My Years with Ayn Rand* (Boston: Houghton Mifflin Company, 1989), 233.

11. Dinesh D'Souza, *The Roots of Obama's Rage* (Washington, D.C.: Regnery Publishing, 2010), 198.

12. GRITtv interview on Real Clear Politics, http://www.real clearpolitics.com/video/2011/03/02/moore_on_wealthy _peoples_money_thats_not_theirs_thats_a_national_re source_its_ours.html (Accessed March 2, 2011).

13. *Avatar* (2009 film), Wikipedia, http://en.wikipedia.org /wiki/Avatar_%282009_film%29.

14. Bertrand Russell, *Principles of Social Reconstruction* (Charleston, S.C.: Nabu Press, 2010).

15. Marcus Tullius Cicero, The Virginian, http://moneyrunner .blogspot.com/2006/09/nation-can-survive-its-fools-and -even.html (Accessed May 19, 2011).

16. Thomas Paine, *Common Sense* (New York: Tribeca Books, 2011).

7. Is It Too Late?

1. Aldous Huxley, *Brave New World* (New York: Harper & Row, 1932, 1946).
2. Alain de Botton, *The Consolations of Philosophy* (New York: Vintage Books, 2000).
3. Review of *Animal Spirits: How Human Psychology Drives the Economy, and Why It Matters for Global Capitalism Daily*, Daily Kos, March 23, 2011, http://forums.eslcafe.com/korea/viewtopic.php?p=2603273.
4. F. A. Hayek, *The Road to Serfdom* (Chicago: The University of Chicago Press, 1944, 2007).

8. The Perpetual, Titanic Struggle

1. Thomas L. Friedman, "Who Will Tell the People?" *New York Times*, May 4, 2008.
2. Henry Ford II speech to the University of Chicago Business School Management Conference, 1979, http://www.chicagobooth.edu/faculty/selectedpapers/sp54.pdf (Accessed May 18, 2011).
3. Frank Chodorov, *The Income Tax: Root of All Evil* (Old Greenwich, Conn.: The Devin-Adair Company, 1954).

INDEX

Index

Index

Index

287

Index

288

Index

Index

Index

Printed in the United States
By Bookmasters